NASTY NATURE

Scholastic Children's Books,
Euston House, 24 Eversholt Street,
London, NW1 1DB, UK

A division of Scholastic Ltd
London ~ New York ~ Toronto ~ Sydney ~ Auckland
Mexico City ~ New Delhi ~ Hong Kong

Published by Scholastic Ltd, 2016

Text © Nick Arnold, 2016
(except text on pages 34–37, 74–75, 86–87 © Tony De Saulles)
Illustration © Tony De Saulles, 2016

ISBN 978 1 407 17089 3

Printed and bound in the UK

Some of the material in this publication has previously been published in the
Horrible Science books © Nick Arnold and Tony De Saulles

Horrible Science® is a registered trademark of Scholastic Ltd.

CONTENTS

Introduction **5**

The Beastly Basics **6**

Odd One Out **10**

Little and Large Facts **12**

Weird Wildlife Quiz **13**

Gifted Gorillas **14**

Awful Animals **16**

Awful Animal Lifestyles **18**

Savage Sharks **20**

Crafty Crocodiles **28**

The Art of Horrible Science **34**

Sinister Snakes **38**

Spot the Difference **45**

Cruel Creatures Wordsearch **46**

Beware of the Bears **48**

Cruel Big Cats **56**

Horrible Hunters **62**

Stunning Sense Stats **68**

Good Parents Award **70**

Pigeon Power **72**

Don't Get in a Flap **74**

Ugly Bugs **76**

Irritating Insects **78**

At Home with the Mites **84**

Bugs and Slugs **86**

Slimy Snails and Ugly Slugs **88**

Burglar Bugs **92**

Awesome Ants **94**

Barmy Bees **98**

Scary Skies **104**

Sinister Spiders **106**

Ugly Bugs vs Horrible Humans **112**

Answers **116**

Index **122**

Nick Arnold wrote his first book aged eight on a giant sheet of printing paper. It was a scary story – just the sort he loved. On leaving university he worked as a science editor and discovered a new love of science. Then, twenty years ago, Nick found he could combine his passions for science and scary stories in the *Horrible Science* series. Ever since, Nick has been busy writing *Horrible Science* books and performing *Horrible Science* shows from China to Mexico. Among his other claims to fame, Nick saved his local library from closure and then rebuilt it. He also founded and directed the Appledore Book Festival and discovered a lost Viking battlefield and a lost Norman battlefield.

Tony De Saulles was working as a freelance designer in 1995 when Scholastic came across his 'horrible humour' and thought it might work well with the new *Horrible Science* series they were planning. This enabled Tony to fulfil his dream of becoming a full-time illustrator. He loves working with children and has held *Horrible Science* drawing workshops at all the big book festivals in the UK as well as in Dubai, India, China and France. In May 2015 he held his biggest-ever workshop, drawing with 1,400 children in the main tent at the Hay Festival. Tony is very excited about the *Horrible Science* TV series on ITV!

INTRODUCTION

Planet Earth has a stunning secret, and you and me and everyone you know is part of it. Because Planet Earth is the only planet we know that has ANIMALS. And we're not talking about the odd worm either.

Planet Earth – our home – has LOTS of animals. In fact almost every part of our planet is crawling and wriggling and squirming and flapping and buzzing and running and leaping with life. (And we're all part of the secret because we're alive too!)

There are creatures big and small – and terribly tiny – and they're all busy doing wild stuff like eating each other or trying not to get eaten. *Nasty Nature* is about them all and it's especially about their horrible habits – the stuff you really want to read. So let's get going – we've got a whole planet to explore but we'll start off with a few beastly basics ...

THE BEASTLY BASICS

300 years ago, scientists had an appallingly difficult problem. Explorers kept discovering freaky new kinds of animals – but how should scientists go about listing this huge variety of new creatures?

It was a toughie. A Swedish scientist called Carl Linnaeus (1707–1778) set out to sort all the plants and animals in the world into some kind of logical order. But Carl had his work cut out. There's an enormous variety of animals in the world. And thousands more were being discovered every year in unlikely places.

BET YOU NEVER KNEW!

There are currently about 10,000,000,000,000,000, 000,000,000,000,000,000 (that's 10 billion, trillion, trillion) animals on Earth (give or take a few million) and they come in all shapes and sizes.

Not a bad sort

Here are the main classes that Linnaeus divided animals into. Now where do you fit in?

CNIDARIA (ni-dare-ee-uh) – 11,000+ species

No, these aren't sci-fi aliens – they just look that way. They live in the sea and their bodies consist of a sort of stomach with tentacles armed with thousands of stinging cells. Nasty examples include jellyfish, sea anemones and corals.

WIBBLE WOBBLE — JELLYFISH

ECHINODERMS (eck-hi-no-derms) – 7,000+ species

These freaky creatures also hang out in the sea. They have hard, often spiky skin. Their legs are hollow tubes arranged around a central area. Eerie examples include starfish and sea urchins.

WAVE WAGGLE — SEA URCHIN

CRUSTACEA (crus-taysh-she-a) – 52,000+ species

Crustacea also have skeletons on the outside of their bodies. These are tough shells that would give an attacker toothache if it tried to bite them. Crunchy examples include crabs, lobsters and barnacles.

SNAP! SNAP! — LOBSTER

ARACHNIDS (arack-nids) – 73,000+ species

The bad news: most of this class are spiders. Erk! The worse news: some are scorpions. Arachnids have their head and thorax (the middle bits) of their bodies joined together. Scorpions have a nasty poisonous sting in their tails but that doesn't stop people in Thailand enjoying roast scorpion. They have 6-12 eyes, eight jointed legs, two pincers and two grasping claws – oh, and I nearly forgot – a nasty poisonous sting in their tails. Some like playing sneaky tricks on humans – like hiding in their shoes!

SHUFFLE SCUTTLE — SCORPION

FISH – 28,000+ species

Most fish have bony skeletons – so when you eat one you can end up with a face full of bones. Other fish such as sharks have gristly skeletons instead. Fish live in water (surprise, surprise) and take dissolved air from the water through the gills in the side of their heads. Most fish are covered in scales and use fins to swim. Well, they're better than water wings.

SLIDE SLITHER — EEL

AMPHIBIA – 6,000+ species

Amphibia are cold-blooded. That doesn't mean that they're pitiless and ruthless killers, although many are. No, "cold-blooded" means they heat up and cool down with their surroundings. They have four legs and their skin is thin and slimy. The name amphibia means "double-lives" in Greek. And frogs and toads do live a double-life.

CROAK!

FROG

REPTILES – 8,200+ species

Reptiles are cold-blooded too, and covered in scales. They have small brains for their size and their legs stick out of the sides of their bodies so they have to crawl around. (Unless they're snakes who slither about instead.) Young reptiles are hatched from eggs. (Don't try eating them for breakfast though.)

LICK!

PLOD   **PLOD**

CHAMELEON   TORTOISE

BIRDS – 10,000+ species

Birds have two legs, a pair of wings and a horny beak. (Bet you bought this just to find that out!) Their bodies are covered with feathers – made from keratin – that's the same stuff as your fingernails. Young birds hatch from eggs laid by their mums. That's if the eggs don't get poached and guzzled for breakfast first.

PECK PECK PECK

COCK-A-DOODLE-DOO

QUACK QUACK

WOODPECKER   COCKEREL   DUCK

MAMMALS – 5,400 species

Mammals are warm-blooded* and most of them live on land and can't fly. Baby mammals are born alive rather than as eggs and they are nourished on milk supplied by their mums. And guess what – we're mammals too. Yes, humans belong to this class.

GOOD BOY

WOOF!

MAN   DOG

*This means that their blood is kept warm because their body is covered with fur or fat to keep the cold out. It's not the same as being "hot-blooded" – that's when someone keeps losing their temper and getting into fights.

Beastly basics quiz

From vertebrates to invertebrates, there are an eye-watering 50 million species on Earth. Don't worry – we're not going to ask you to name them! What you need to do is cast your eye over these frighteningly fiendish questions about our beastly buddies (complete with curiously kind clues)...

1 What's the proper name for meat-scoffing animals?
(CLUE: They'd love chilli con carne)

2 How does the cute little fieldfare bird protect its nest? *(CLUE: You'd need a good wash afterwards!)*

3 What do scary scavengers such as vultures like to chow down on?
(CLUE: They're not worried about 'best before' dates!)

4 Which fearsome reptile has a nerve-shredding roar like 'distant thunder'? *(CLUE: They get snappy when hungry)*

5 Why do snakes pick up sound waves from the ground?
(CLUE: They can't wear glasses)

6 Why do hippos ooze a red, oily substance from their skin?
(CLUE: Look up for an answer!)

7 What kind of bear eats more meat than any other wild animal? *(CLUE: They might keep it in the freezer)*

8 What would happen to plant-eating animals if all the world's meat-eating creatures died?
(CLUE: It's dead simple)

See page 116 for answers

ODD ONE OUT

Can you spot which of these colourful chameleons is the odd one out?

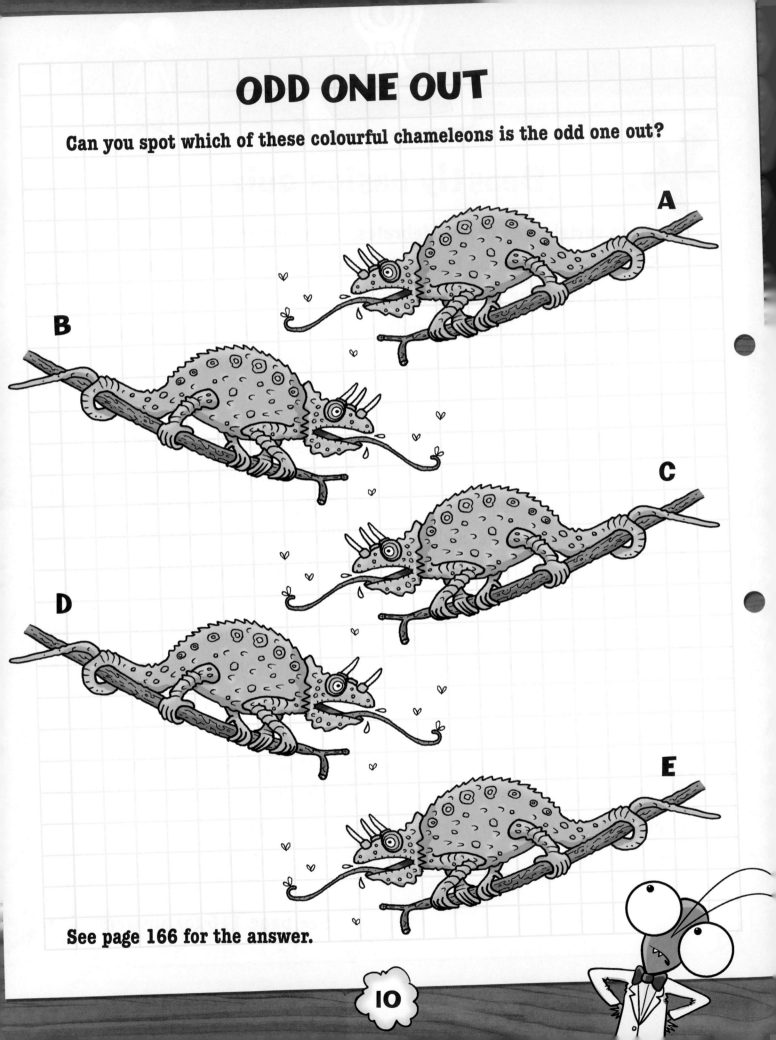

See page 166 for the answer.

Little and LARGE FACTS

SIZE OF AN ELEPHANT COMPARED WITH A BLUE WHALE

The largest animal that has ever lived is the blue whale. This creature can grow to 33 metres long and weigh 80 tonnes. That's 24 times the size of an elephant and even bigger than the biggest dinosaur. Inside the blue whale there are over 8,500 litres of blood protected by a layer of fat 61 cm thick. But here's a nasty thought: since 1900 human hunters have brought at least 378,000 of these stupendous creatures to a horrible end.

Compare that with ... Helena's hummingbird.
It's only 5.7 cm from bill to tail and weighs a mere 2 grams. This tiny scrap of a creature lives off sweet, sticky nectar from flowers.

HUMMING BIRD

TUM TE TUM, DUM DI DOO DAH

BIRD HUMMING

The Marshall Islands goby is a tiddler of a fish that lives in the Pacific Ocean. It is only 1.27 cm long.

AH! A WORM!

ACTUAL SIZE

A tiny fish sounds a bit weird but some creatures are Weird with a capital W. Which of these beasts is too wacky to be true?

Weird wildlife quiz

1 The storsjoodjuret is an ugly looking long-necked reptile that skulks around in Lake Storsjön in Sweden. It's between 10–20 metres long. **TRUE/FALSE?**

2 There's a type of bird with a horn on its head like a unicorn. It's called a "horned screamer". **TRUE/FALSE?**

3 The Jack Dempsey fish is named after a famous American boxer. This small South American freshwater fish got its name because it enjoys ramming into other fish and stealing their eggs. **TRUE/FALSE?**

4 The Malaysian two-headed bat has a lump on its back that looks just like an extra head. This fools owls that attempt to bite the bat's head off in mid-air. **TRUE/FALSE?**

5 There's a type of snake that can fly short distances. **TRUE/FALSE?**

6 The Indian climbing perch is a fish that climbs trees. **TRUE/FALSE?**

WHAT ARE YOU DOING?

TREE FISHING

7 The Iberian "singing" goat is an excellent mimic. (That's the posh name for someone who copies voices.) It has been known to imitate the yodelling calls of local mountaineers! **TRUE/FALSE?**

8 There's a creature that hangs out in Australian rivers with a bill like a duck and fur like a beaver. It lays eggs like a bird and has poisonous spines like a lizard. **TRUE/FALSE?**

See page 116 for answers

GIFTED GORILLAS

Gorillas at Frankfurt Zoo, Germany, enjoy watching TV. What's their favourite viewing?

a) Soap operas

b) Wildlife documentaries about other gorillas

c) Sports programmes, including the football results

Gorilla Language

Ever wanted to gossip with a gorilla? Here's a few words of gorilla language to get you going!

WRAAGH! = DANGER!

GRUNT = BEHAVE YOURSELF (used by adult gorillas towards their youngsters).

A BARKING HOOTING SOUND = I'M CURIOUS.

HOO, HOO, HOO = KEEP OUT!

BEATING CHEST = I'M BOSS.

HOO, HOO, HOO!

WRAAGH!

BET YOU NEVER KNEW!

Animals raised by humans sometimes keep pets. One of the apes taught to "speak" using sign language in America, was Koko the gorilla. Now Koko was happy living with researcher Dr "Penny" Patterson. But the gorilla had one wish. More than anything else – she wanted a kitten of her own. So in 1984 kind-hearted Dr Patterson gave her one.

Koko called her new pet "All Ball". She treated All Ball as her baby and even dressed it in cute little hats and scraps of material. Koko often tried to get the kitten to tickle her. (The gorilla enjoyed being tickled by her human friends.) And when the kitten was well-behaved Koko signed that it was a "soft good cat". Altogether now – Ahhhh. But if you like happy endings don't read the bit below.

Soon after, All Ball was run over and killed. Boo hoo! Poor Koko was heart-broken and nothing could cheer her up until Dr Patterson bought her another kitten.

ANSWER: **c)** Obviously they thought that the games were the real monkey business!

AWFUL ANIMALS

For an animal, every day brings its dangers. Brainy bunny Mr Fluffy has agreed to give us a rabbit's eye view of life in the wild and even show us his photograph album. Uh-oh – these scientists don't look too happy...

BUT RABBITS DON'T HAVE PHOTO ALBUMS!

GRRR — THIS IS GETTING SILLY!

HE'S NOT AS BRAINY AS US!

OH, LIGHTEN UP, THIS IS SUPPOSED TO BE FUN!

THE HORRIBLE SCIENCE INTERVIEW

Mr Fluffy the rabbit tells it like it is...

Horrible Science: So what's it like being a rabbit?

Mr Fluffy: Well, like all animals, I just want a quiet life and all the carrots I can eat.

Me eating carrots.

Horrible Science: Er, I'm not sure about the carrots... Anything else on your mind?

Mr F: You bet — I don't want to get eaten. Trouble is, loads of creatures want to eat me.

Here's a photo of when I nearly got snatched by a hawk...

Here's when a snake sneaked up on me...

I must say it helps to have eyes on the side of my head so I can spot anything creeping up on me. And it's lucky I'm a fast runner!

And here's me being chased by a fox...

Horrible Science: Your life must be pretty dangerous...

Mr F: Well, it's even worse if I fall sick... And then there's the blood-sucking fleas that live in my fur.

Me feeling flea-bitten and unwell.

Horrible Science (scratching): Ouch — I've just met them! Is there anything more you'd like out of life, Mr Fluffy?

Mr F: I want to father lots of baby bunnies ... and I could do with a packet of flea powder.

BET YOU NEVER KNEW!

1 Life is especially dangerous for baby animals. If they're left by their parents, they can starve or get eaten by another creature.

2 Some baby animals are killed by their own brothers and sisters.

• Baby eagles push their brothers' and sisters' eggs out of the nest before they hatch. That way there'll be more food for them.

• Baby hyenas fight even when they're new-born and they can kill each other when they're bigger. Of course your family isn't quite this bad... Or is it?

And now for three facts that will turn you into an instant zoologist. Oops, silly me. I bet you don't know what I'm talking about...

A **zoologist** is an animal scientist.

A **habitat** is the place an animal lives in.

Three animal-tastic facts

(don't turn the page until you've read them)...

1 Every animal in the world has a habitat, where it finds food and shelter.

2 Animals depend on one another...

OOER!

FOX = MEAT-EATING ANIMAL.

Meat-eating animals depend on plant-eating animals for food. And plant-eaters depend on meat-eaters. By eating weak and sick rabbits, foxes ensure that only the strongest bunnies get to mate, and this breeds strong, healthy rabbit families. And by keeping rabbit numbers down, the foxes stop the rabbits from guzzling all the grass and starving to death.

3 Scientists describe the complicated feeding links between animals as a food web...

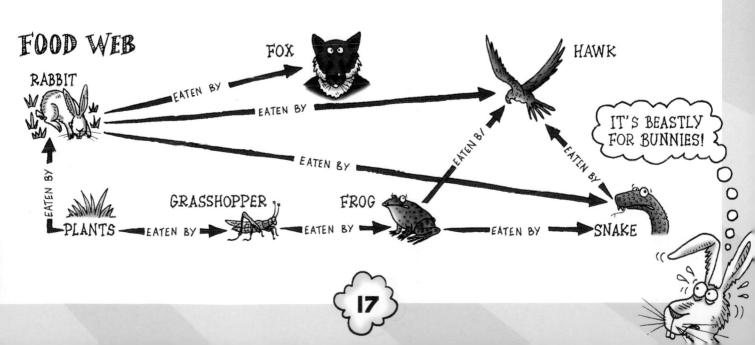

FOOD WEB

RABBIT — EATEN BY → FOX

EATEN BY → HAWK

EATEN BY

EATEN BY

IT'S BEASTLY FOR BUNNIES!

EATEN BY

PLANTS ← EATEN BY → GRASSHOPPER — EATEN BY → FROG — EATEN BY → SNAKE

AWFUL ANIMAL LIFESTYLES

Every animal wants much the same things as Mr Fluffy – food, safety and babies. But, as you're about to find out, every animal has its own way of achieving these aims…

Finding food

Every type of food has its drawbacks…

• Plants are easy to catch (they don't run away) but you need to eat a lot of plants to feed yourself. The cellulose is tough to digest – and that means you need a big gut to eat it. Plant-eaters such as cows and rabbits have bacteria in their guts to rot plants so they can be digested. So does the hoatzin bird. This bulging Brazilian bird has a big stomach and spends its time eating and burping to get rid of the gas the bacteria make.

• Animal meat is easier to digest and contains more energy, but you've got to catch your dinner first.

And you need super-senses…

> *Pic of me dripping*
>
> *The secret diary of an echidna*
>
> *Dear Diary*
> *It's been another tough beetle-grub-hunting day. The little blighters hide underground – what I'd do without my super-sensitive snout is anyone's guess! Thanks to my snout I can sense electrical forces in the grubs' muscles and dig them up for dinner. Pity my nifty nose can only work when it's wet and drips snot all the time. I could really do with a hankie – ATISHOO!*
>
> *DRIP!*

Staying safe

Animals try to hide or run from larger, fiercer animals, but if they get cornered, they have to fight back or act dead…

The secret diary of a hog-nosed snake

Dear Diary

Today was the worst day of my life! There I was happily snaking about when a dog leapt on me. Luckily I'm a good actor so I gave him my famous cobra impression – rearing up and hissing. It was quite a performance, if I say so myself, luvvies! But the miserable mutt just barked. Time for Plan B, I thought, and rolled over and played dead. Being dead is one of my best-ever acts, and to make it even more life-like, er, I mean death-like, I squirted smelly juice as if I was rotting. That foiled foolish Fido and he slunk off... I reckon it must be worth an Oscar!

Me doing my cobra thing

Having kids

All animals have to produce young or their species will die out. There are two ways to make sure as many babies survive as possible...

• Produce lots of babies and don't look after them. The strongest will survive without help and having more babies means more should make it. Examples include fish and frogs.

• Produce a few babies but care for them. That way there's less chance of losing any. Examples include mammals such as humans.

But even animals that care for their young sometimes put them to work...

The secret diary of a naked mole rat

This is me (naked)

Dear Diary

I hate my life! I mean, it's bad enough looking like a sausage with fangs ... but Mum gives me and my brothers and sisters a hard time! She's always biting us and making us work all day in our tunnel garden. Today I had to chew roots and plant them in the soil so they will regrow. And afterwards I had to feed my baby brothers and sisters with my own poo. I wish I was a real rat – then I'd bite back!

SAVAGE SHARKS

I bet you can't wait to get your teeth into some savagely shocking shark stories... but this is a respectable educational book so we're going to have a few facts instead. (Oh, all right – I'll tell you the bloody bits on page 23.)

Angry animals fact file

NAME OF CREATURE: Great white shark

TYPE OF ANIMAL: Fish

DIET: Carnivore – eats fish and mammals such as cute seals and dolphins and the odd not-so-cute human.

NUMBER OF PEOPLE KILLED*: Great white sharks kill fewer than two people per year. (On average, all types of shark only kill about 12 people a year.)

WHERE THEY LIVE: Cool oceans all around the world. For some strange reason they like to hang around islands where seals live. Any guesses why?

SIZE: Females are larger than males and they can be up to 4.5 metres long. Some great whites grow to over 6 metres and can weigh 3 tonnes.

* All figures are estimates and may vary from year to year.

FEARSOME FEATURES:

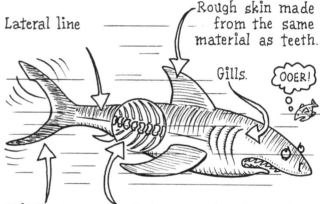

Lateral line

Rough skin made from the same material as teeth.

Gills.

OOER!

Tail beats from side to side.

Skeleton made of cartilage (it's the same stuff that makes up your nose and ears).

BET YOU NEVER KNEW!
In 2003 scientists in Canada found that fish send messages by farting bubbles. Herring keep in touch at night using high-pitched bottom burps. No one knows if sharks have musical bottoms but you're welcome to find out ... if you dare!

OOPS – PARDON!

Four facts

that not a lot of people know about great white sharks

1 Great white sharks hatch from eggs whilst still inside their mums. They keep alive by eating unhatched eggs. That's right – they gobble up their unborn brothers and sisters.

2 Once it's born, a baby great white shark has to hide from adult sharks who might try to eat it. Even the baby's mum might try to munch it. And you thought you had it tough…

3 As a great white shark grows older it gets greyer on top and bigger round the middle – just like some humans! Of course, the sharks are fairly grey on top already – the colour helps them to blend in with the dark sea when seen from above.

4 A great white shark has a "belly button" … on its throat! It's the mark where the yolk of the egg is connected to its body.

Ruthless relatives

So you thought your relatives were bad? Wait 'til you meet some of the other human-killers in the shark family! They're not into happy families, but they might want to play "SNAP" with you...

BULL SHARK

Size: 2.1 to 3.5 metres long.

Lives: Warm seas close to coasts; sometimes swims up rivers.

Dreadful danger: The brutal bull shark chomps any humans it finds in the river. This antisocial habit makes it a bigger killer than the great white.

TIGER SHARK

Size: 3 to 6 metres long.

Lives: Warm oceans, just like the ones people like to swim in.

Dreadful danger: The terrible tiger shark isn't too fussy about food and will happily eat a human. This gives a totally new meaning to the phrase "feeding the fish".

Now, I suppose you're wondering what it's like to be attacked by one of these savage sharks. Well, it's no fun at all... Take a look at this shocking shark story – this is how the paper might have reported it. In bite-sized chunks, naturally...

The Matawan News
12 July 1916

CRACKPOT CAPTAIN'S SHARK SCARE STORY!

Captain Thomas Cottrell says he's spotted a shark in the creek just 100 metres from our town. "I saw its dark grey shape in the water!" puffed the potty pensioner as he hurried into town to alert locals. But everyone laughed at the oddball old-timer.

Capt. Cottrell

The News says...
WHAT A FISHY TALE! So old Captain Cottrell's seen a shark? Like heck he has! Matawan folk won't be panicked by this far-fetched fishy tale. Our town is 16 km from the sea and the creek is too shallow for sharks. So grab your towels and enjoy a dip! Yes – let's ignore that strange old sea dog!

The Matawan News
14 July 1916

STOP THESE SHOCK SHARK SLAYINGS!

Matawan is reeling after the savage shark attacks that killed two local lads and injured another. First the fearsome fish seized young Lester Stilwell when he was swimming with friends. At first no one knew it was a shark, and when have-a-go hero Stanley Fisher tried to rescue Lester's body the fearsome fish bit Fisher's leg off. He died later in hospital.

As terror gripped the town, men piled into boats and dropped dynamite into the creek to blast the shark to bits.

But the shark bit back. As Joseph Dunn and his friends tried to flee the water – the savage shark chomped the young lad's leg.

Readers' letters

From Mary Anderson

Dear Editor
I warned Stanley Fisher. I told him it could have been a shark that got young Lester but that poor foolish boy took no notice! Speaking as Stanley's old teacher I wish that young people would show more respect and not get themselves eaten by giant fish! It didn't happen in my day!

The News Says...
SORRY READERS! We would like to apologize for the misprint in the News of two days ago. When we said "enjoy a dip" we actually meant to say "that shark's gonna let rip!"

The facts of this story are true, but modern experts aren't too sure what species of shark carried out the attack. Some sharks were caught near the scene but no one knew which one was the killer. Most people blamed a great white, which had bones in its stomach, but a bull shark may have been the guilty fish.

And while we're talking about being eaten by a shark you might be feeling a trifle peckish. If so, here's a revolting recipe to relish…

THE HORRIBLE SCIENCE COOK BOOK
Shark Stomach Soup

This soup is based on items that were really found in sharks' stomachs…

INGREDIENTS
A horse's head
Bits of bicycle
A human arm
One dog's backbone
One whole goat (make sure it's 100 per cent dead!)
Shark's stomach juices
Salt and pepper

WHAT YOU NEED
A big pot
A clothes peg for your nose – your soup is going to pong!

A supply of sick bags

WHAT YOU DO
1. Stir the ingredients in the big pot.
Or you could pour them into a shark's stomach.
2. Heat gently until the sickening stink is so bad you can't bear it any more.
3. Serve your soup before the neighbours complain and enjoy the sight of all your friends throwing up.
4. Pour the rest of the soup down the toilet.
5. Go into hiding.

BET YOU NEVER KNEW!
The human arm belonged to an Australian gangster named James Smith. It turned up inside a tiger shark in 1935. One of Smith's crooked mates confessed to killing the criminal and dumping his body in a metal box. He cut off Smith's arm because it stuck out of the box…

Savage shark survival quiz

Naturally you're far too sensible to be caught by a great white shark, aren't you? And that's why you've just been signed up for this cruel quiz... You're having the holiday to end all holidays – but will it prove to be the end of YOU?

WARNING!
IF YOU LOSE THE QUIZ YOU GET EATEN BY A SHARK!!!

1 Where's the safest place to swim?

SHARK ISLAND
POPULATION 136 135 134

a) Next to the Shark Island Fishing Competition – I can watch it underwater.

b) Next to the seals. I'll love playing with them.

c) Close to the lifeguard's hut.

GRORK!

2 What's the safest thing to wear?

a) My bright yellow stripy swimming cozzie (it'll scare the sharks away) plus my lucky charm for extra good fortune.

b) A suit of armour.

c) An ordinary swimming costume.

3 What's the best anti-shark protection?

a) A bottle of shampoo.

b) My shark-blaster bomb-stick.

c) My pet dolphin.

ANTI SHARK

4 Anything else you've forgotten?

a) My surfboard – I could surf a wave and escape the shark.

b) A dead sheep to feed the shark with – that way it won't be hungry for me.

c) Nothing.

5 The shark attacks you – what's the best thing to do?

a) Reason with it in a calm but firm tone of voice.

b) Stick my finger in its eye or punch its nose.

c) Scream very loudly and wave my arms in the air.

See pages 116–117 for the answers

DEATH ON THE OCEAN WAVE

Visiting aliens Oddblob the Blurb and Slobslime the Snottie decided to unwind on an ocean cruise, but they reckoned without the sharks and jellyfish...

Did you know?

If you're attacked by a great white shark you could try punching its nose or poking its eyes. Victims are also advised to shout and wave both hands for help. If you wave one hand people tend to wave back.

In 2007 Australian diver Eric Nerhus was swallowed headfirst by a great white shark. Luckily for Eric, the shark's gigantic jaws scrunched his lead-weighted vest. Eric poked the shark's eye until the fearsome fish let him go.

In 1998 a nurse shark bit a teenager in Florida and hung on so tightly that the shark had to go to hospital with the boy.

Dolphins hunt fish using rapid bursts of high-pitched sound. The dolphins follow the echoes bouncing off the fish. Human brains aren't fast enough to make sense of each sound pulse and all we make out is a teeth-jangling screech.

In 2006 two dolphins in Fushun, China, ate plastic in their pool. Vets couldn't help the ailing animals but then the world's tallest man, Bao Xishun showed up. Bao shoved his long arm into the dolphins' stomachs to pull out the plastic.

Some people think that seals cry. In fact tears do trickle down a seal's cheeks but they're designed to keep its eyes moist.

WEEP!

Mating hammerhead sharks cruise in huge schools made up of hundreds of hungry hammerheads. You'd best stay out of the water when they're around.

Ask your teacher "Is the Portuguese man o' war a jellyfish?" With luck they'll say "yes" and you can tell them off for being wrong. In fact it's a jelly-like animal called a siphonophore.

WRONG!

CRAFTY CROCODILES

The creature in this section could put you off messing about on the river for life – well, your life won't last five minutes if you get too close. It's true! Just look at these crucial crocodile facts…

Angry animals fact file

NAME OF CREATURE: Nile crocodile

TYPE OF ANIMAL: Reptile

DIET: Carnivore – eats fish, mammals, birds and anything it can scrunch. Crocs only need to feed once a week – but they can still kill a human.

NUMBER OF PEOPLE KILLED: Several hundred per year.

WHERE THEY LIVE: Rivers and lakes in Africa and Madagascar.

SIZE: Up to 4.88 metres long. The bigger crocs are the older ones but luckily they lose their teeth with age. Still, you could be "gummed" to death.

FEARSOME FEATURES:

Hard palate between mouth and nose protects croc's squishy brain from a victim's kick in the gob.

Yes, crocs do have a heart – and it's not too different from yours!

K-PLOOP!

X-RAY VIEW

Scaly waterproof skin

SNAP!

Waterproof eggs

Flaps in nose, ears and throat keep mucky river water out. These are vital since crocs have no lips to seal their mouths.

Powerful tail can break a deer's legs.

BET YOU NEVER KNEW!
Most reptiles don't have voices, but crocs do. Their roars sound like distant thunder – I'd hate to hear them singing in the bath first thing in the morning!

Ruthless relatives

ALLIGATOR

Size: Males are up to 3.66 metres long.

Lives: South and Central America, southern USA, China.

Dreadful danger: American alligators are relaxed reptiles when it comes to humans. In the USA they only kill about one person a year. Mind you, that doesn't make them safe. If you bathed in their rivers they'd probably turn your bath-time into barf-time.

SALTWATER CROCODILE (known to its friends as "saltie").

Size: Up to 6 metres long.

Lives: Rivers and coasts in southern Asia and the Pacific including Australia. They've been spotted up to 970 km from land.

Dreadful danger: These angry animals reckon their stretch of the river belongs to them and trespassers will be eaten. We're talking about two people per year in Australia and many more in the rest of the world.

SPOT THE DIFFERENCE COMPETITION
Can you spot THREE differences between these pictures?

Answers on page 117

Speaking personally, I don't think it's terribly sensible to wrestle with caymans or crocodiles. And if you tried to wrestle with these celebrity crocs you might end up missing some vital body bits...

Top of the crocs

WHAH!

At number 5...

SWEETHEART

(Yes, that's an odd name for a huge flesh-eating reptile but read on and all will be revealed.)

Home: Sweet's Look-out Billabong, Australia. (Told you!)

Hobbies: Crunching outboard motors.

Fate: Apart from biting boats, Sweetheart never did anyone any harm but sadly the saltie (that means saltwater croc, remember?) died when scientists tried to knock him out to move him away from people.

SOLOMON

Home: A wildlife park in Australia.

Hobbies: Eating and basking in the sun.

Fate: One day in 1997, wildlife-park worker Karla Bradl was showing Solomon the saltie to some tourists when the cunning croc chomped her leg. Karla's dad (the park boss) jabbed the croc's eyes until it let go and luckily Solomon was old and partly toothless. In fact, Karla had just said: "If I ever get grabbed, I'd rather it be this one!"

At number 4...

DRIBBLE!

I expect Solomon felt a bit down in the mouth. But you'll be pleased to hear that Karla's dad refused to let Solomon be killed saying "...he wouldn't bite anything with bones in it." Except his daughter of course!

KWENA

Home: Okovango Swamp, Botswana, Africa.

Hobbies: Gobbling goats (and people).

Fate: When Kwena was killed in 1968, the 5.8 metre killer croc had two goats, half a donkey and half a woman in its stomach.

We've nearly reached Number One – but first...

BUJANG SENANG

Home: Lupar River, Sarawak, Borneo.

Hobbies: Football and eating people. (To be honest, I'm not too sure if the croc even liked football, but the local team named itself after the revolting reptile.)

Fate: In the 1980s and 1990s this crafty croc crunched dozens of people but always managed to hide from hunters. And a witch doctor's bid to catch the croc by magic spells spelled failure.

AND NOW FOR THE BIG NUMBER 1 – AND IT REALLY IS BIG...

GUSTAVE

Home: Burundi, Africa.

Hobbies: Scaring hippos and eating people.

Fate: Terrified locals claimed the gigantic 1 tonne croc had eaten over 300 people. In March 2003 an international team of scientists tried to trap the croc in a giant cage or using spring traps. But the crafty croc dodged the traps ... until one day he disappeared, never to be seen again. Maybe he'd gone to a croc-and-roll concert...

I hope you're hungry for crafty croc and artful alligator attack facts because here's a cruel quiz to chew over. My mate Honest Bob has six facts – but beware! Bob's as dodgy as a second-hand dodgem car. The facts get more and more freaky. Can you spot where the facts stop being true and start being false? Over to you, Bob! (See page 117 for the answers.)

HONEST BOB'S "CAN YOU BELIEVE IT?" QUIZ

TRUE/FALSE

1. In 2001 a Florida alligator tried to eat ... a live horse!
2. In 2001 a camper in Australia woke to find himself in bed with ... a crocodile!
3. In 2002 an African crocodile was bitten by ... a man!
4. In 2004 a group of children took an alligator ... to school by bus!
5. In 2005 a teacher was attacked on the toilet by ... an alligator that lived in the sewer!
6. In 2005 scientists found a fossil crocodile ... with wings!

All this talk of ruthless reptiles raises quite a queasy question.

How exactly do crocs and alligators attack humans?

Oh dear, I'm sure you don't want to know –

it's really very gruesome…

BUT WE DO!

Well, I've got a uneasy feeling that our top TV naturalist Will D Beest is about to find out.

Ouch, I bet that hurt, Will! When Australian wildlife ranger Charlie Finn was attacked by a saltie, the cruel croc grabbed his arm. Charlie said later: "I heard the sounds of bones crunching. It was pretty horrible." The croc went into a death roll, but luckily it let go of Charlie's chewed arm.

Crunch-time for crocs

Still, this is all scientifically fascinating, and whilst Will's recovering in hospital, we've asked the croc that did the damage to tell us about his eating habits…

We crocodiles drown our prey — including humans. That way they don't fight back and we can guzzle them at leisure. Like sharks, we can't chew. We rip off bits of body and gulp them down. Sometimes we leave the body to rot until it's soft and squishy enough to bite off bits more easily. The acid in our stomach is strong enough to dissolve bones.

Hey — why's that crocodile getting all the attention?

Cos he's more interesting than you!

Ruthless relatives

Here are a few more poisonous snakes you wouldn't want to wake up with...

A CRATE OF KRAITS

COMMON KRAIT (Plus 12 other species)

Size: Up to 1.8 metres long.

Lives: India and southern Asia.

Danger-rating: The Indian common krait likes nothing better than crawling into your bed whilst you're asleep. Unfortunately its bite contains a deadly nightmare nerve poison... Sweet dreams!

FEELING RATTLED?

QUIVER!

RATTLESNAKE

Size: Up to 2.4 metres.

Lives: North America.

Danger-rating: There are 29 species and they're all poisonous. They kill fewer than 15 people in the USA every year, though.

SEA SNAKE

Size: Up to 90 cm long.

Lives: Indian and Pacific Oceans.

Danger-rating: Rarely bites humans although it does enjoy chasing divers. Its bite is the most poisonous of any snake. Fancy a dip?

SSSSWIM FOR YOUR LIFE!

BLACK MAMBA

Size: Up to 4.3 metres long.

Lives: Africa – south of the Sahara Desert.

Danger-rating: Its poison can kill in 20 minutes. In the 1970s South African snake expert Jack Seale spent weeks sharing a small room with a black mamba. He said the secret of survival was not to move quickly... Lucky he didn't need the toilet in a hurry then.

THE SPITTING COBRA

Size: Up to 2.5 metres long.

Lives: Africa – south of the Sahara desert.

Danger-rating: Low. OK, so if you dried the poison and injected it into 165 humans they'd all die. But this snake spits its poison (how come you knew that already?) and it can't hurt if it lands on your skin. The bad news: if the poison hits your eyes it can dissolve your eyeballs. The very bad news: the snake aims for the eyes. The yikes-I-need-a-clean-pair-of-pants bad news: it's a very good shot.

HEY! IT'S RUDE TO SPIT!

DARE YOU DISCOVER... if you're as accurate as the spitting cobra?

YOU WILL NEED:
- A water pistol (Make sure you fill it with water and not snake poison!)
- An eyeball (If you don't have a spare eyeball here's one we've borrowed. You can trace it and draw it on a piece of card.)
- A measuring tape
- Blu Tack

HURRY UP – I NEED IT BACK!

WHAT YOU DO:

⭐ Stick the eyeball to the wall 1.5 metres up with the Blu Tack (this is best done outside).

⭐ Measure 2.5 metres from the wall.

⭐ Crouch down and try to hit the eyeball with a jet of water.

YOU SHOULD FIND:

This is tricky for you but easy for a sinister spitting cobra.

HORRIBLE HEALTH WARNING!
You should only use water pistols for this experiment and that means NO SPITTING. And no spitting at your pet snake/teacher either!

Is your teacher a herpetologist (that's the posh name for a snake scientist)? If so, they may have a cobra named Colin which they feed small furry animals (so that's what happened to Hamish the school hamster!). Anyway here are some strange snake secrets that they probably don't know...

Seven strange snake secrets

1 Even your most scary school teacher can't out-stare a snake. Snakes can't blink because they don't have eyelids. See-through scales protect their eyes.

2 Ever wondered how sea snakes eat really spiny fish without them getting stuck in their throats? Me neither – but apparently they gulp the fish and then force the spines out through their own bodies. I guess they must be prickly characters!

THEY'RE A PAIN IN THE NECK!

3 It's possible to eat snake eggs. The trick is to choose the smooth ones. The crumpled ones contain baby snakes and their bite can be poisonous. So if you eat the wrong egg you'd best scramble.

4 Although snakes taste smells using their tongues, some species have nostrils too.

5 Snakes take baths. Before they shed their skin they take a dip to make their skin moist. Then they unroll their skin along the length of their body. It's a bit like Will D Beest taking off a sock – but without the cheesy whiff.

PHWOAR!

6 A snake can decide how much poison to give you. The crosser the snake the more you get!

7 And talking about poison, US scientists have found that cottonmouth snake poison is ideal for shifting stubborn stains. Of course it shifts stubborn humans too. Anyone want to test the vile venomous cleaner? If the test goes wrong at least you'd suffer a clean death.

So, how does it feel to be bitten by a poisonous snake – is it really as bad as it sounds?

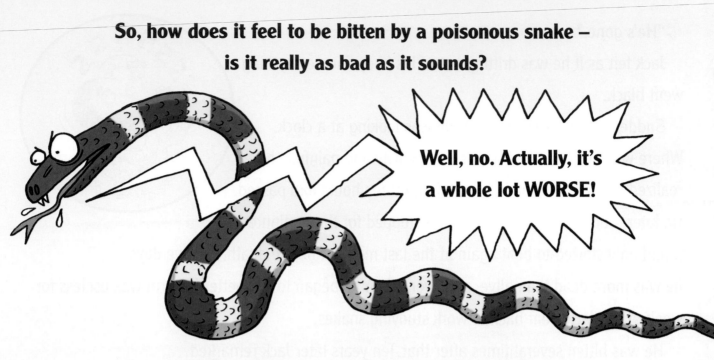

Well, no. Actually, it's a whole lot WORSE!

A snakebite survivor's story

In 1987 British snake expert Jack Corney (1924–2003) was collecting poison from a rattlesnake for scientists to study. Jack knew what he was doing but as he held the snake by the back of its neck the killer creature bit his thumb.

"Don't panic," Jack said to himself grimly. "Freeze your mind." He knew that if he let himself

feel scared, his heart would beat faster and pump the poison more quickly around his body.

Carefully he replaced the snake in its box and wrapped a bandage tightly around his bitten arm. But he was too late. As the poison took hold Jack began to gasp for air. His injured arm swelled to three times its size. The pain was an unspeakable agony. Jack gritted his teeth and rang for help.

In hospital Jack's heart stopped, but he still could hear and feel as the doctors fought for his life. One doctor held Jack's wrist and tried to find a pulse as another stuck a needle in his arm.

"We're losing him," said one doctor.

"He's gone."

Jack felt as if he was drifting out of his body. Then everything went black.

Suddenly Jack's eyes opened. He was looking at a clock. Where was he? What had happened? Slowly and painfully he realized that he was still in hospital and three hours had passed. He later found out that his heart had stopped for three minutes and it had only started to beat again at the last moment before death. For five days he was more dead than alive, and even when he began to get better his arm was useless for weeks. Then Jack went back to work studying snakes.

He was bitten several times after that. Ten years later Jack remarked…

"Some people think I'm mad doing this job…"

Now I wonder why they thought that?

Obviously you don't want to mess about with poisonous snakes – so here are a few snake experts' safety tips, just in case you find yourself in snake country…

EXPERT SNAKE SAFETY TIPS
– don't leave home without them!

1. Always wear long trousers and boots. They protect you against bites from small snakes.

2. Always step on top of logs rather than over them. There may be a snake hiding on the other side.

3. If you see a snake always keep a safe distance – the snake can't strike more than half its length.

4. Make sure the snake has a way to escape.

5. Stay calm – I said DON'T PAAAAAAANIC!

SPOT THE DIFFERENCE

Can you find all 8 differences between these two sinister snakes?

CRUEL CREATURES WORDSEARCH

This quiz asks you to find and draw a line through words hidden in the wordsearch below. The words you'll be looking for are the ones written in CAPITALS in the wild and woolly facts below...

1 The most vicious hunter in the world is said by many biologists to be the short-tailed SHREW (a mouse-like animal) from North America. It has a poisonous bite deadly enough to kill 200 mice.

2 If a CROCODILE attacks you the best thing to do is grip its snout and hold its jaws shut. The muscles that open the croc's mouth are quite weak and even a puny human can hold the mouth shut.

3 The Portuguese man o' war is a type of JELLYFISH. Its sting can stop the nerves working and in the Bahamas and Majorca local people believe that the best treatment is to get someone to pee on your injuries.

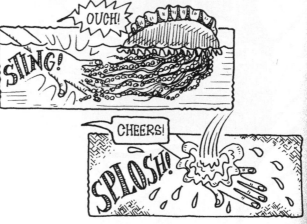

4 The venom of a saw-scaled VIPER stops blood from clotting and contains a chemical that dissolves human flesh. The flesh around a bite from one of these nasties starts to dissolve and bleed uncontrollably and the bitten arm or leg sometimes has to be chopped off.

5 The robber CRAB of the Pacific climbs trees and eats coconuts. This ruthless crab will probably pinch your toes, too.

6 In 1685, a ship was wrecked off the bleak island of North Rona in Scotland. The ship's RATS swam ashore and ate all the islanders' food. Heavy seas prevented the islanders escaping and they all starved to death.

7 The sharp-beaked FINCH of the Galapagos islands eats seeds but it's also a vampire, pecking holes in the wings of nesting sea birds and sucking their blood.

8 The OKAPI (a zebra-like creature that's actually more closely related to the giraffe) can wash its face and ears with its 36 cm (14 inch) tongue. Can you do this?

IT'S TRUE!

Wordsearch

(One point per word, total score eight points.)

```
H  S  I  F  Y  L  L  E  J
B  A  R  C  S  F  E  S  V
C  W  E  R  H  S  A  T  H
L  I  P  A  K  O  K  A  P
E  L  I  D  O  C  O  R  C
J  E  V  H  C  N  I  F  O
```

BEWARE OF THE BEARS

Mr Bottomly has a deeply embarrassing secret...

Mr Bottomly by day

The bear is a crepuscular omnivore, blah, blah...

bear

Mr Bottomly by night

Night, night, Mr Wuffles

OH DEAR, THIS IS SHOCKING

– but a lot of people honestly think bears are cute cuddly teddies. Huh!
If you tried to cuddle a real bear you'd suffer a grisly grizzly fate...

Angry animals fact file

NAME OF CREATURE: Brown bear
(known in North America as the grizzly)

TYPE OF ANIMAL: Mammal

DIET: Bears are omnivores and insectivores. They eat everything – and I mean EVERYTHING! If you don't believe me, just wait 'til you get to page 50!

NUMBER OF PEOPLE KILLED: Less than five a year in the USA.

WHERE THEY LIVE: Wild areas of North America, Russia and Eastern Europe.

SIZE: About 1.3 metres to their big hairy shoulders.

FEARSOME FEATURES:

Sense of smell is 100 times more sensitive than a human's.

Coat can be brown... or black or even blonde. (Best not ask this grizzly if she's a "natural blonde".)

Grumpy bad temper.

GRRR!

"Hump" on back called a roach.

Different types of teeth for biting and slicing meat and chewing plant food.

14 cm claws.

Grizzlies can have two or three cubs every three years.

Powerful legs can run at 50 km per hour.

Ruthless relatives

...AND WE'RE "TREE-MENDOUS" CLIMBERS!

BLACK BEAR

Size: Up to 1.7 metres long (they're smaller than brown bears).

Lives: North American forests.

Danger-rating: They kill a human every five years or so. Because they often live closer to humans they attack us more often than brown bears.

POLAR BEAR

Size: Up to 3 metres tall on their hind legs. Polar bears are the biggest meat-eaters on land. (If you meet one in the dark it won't be all white on the night.)

Lives: On and around the Arctic Ocean.

Danger-rating: On average, polar bears kill a person every three years or so in North America. They kill even more rarely in Russia.

OF COURSE WE'RE THE BIGGEST MEAT-EATERS... THERE AREN'T ANY PLANTS!

QUICK TRUE OR FALSE QUIZ

1 Polar bears are left-handed.

2 In 2003 a polar bear in a zoo in Argentina was dyed pink.

3 Bear brains have a built-in cooling system.

4 Bears don't go to the toilet all winter.

5 Some bears pee whilst doing handstands.

6 Brown bears stink of rotten fish.

7 The best thing to do if you're attacked by a brown bear is climb a tree.

IT MADE ME SEE RED!

IT'S IMPORTANT TO KEEP A COOL HEAD!

OK SO I HAVEN'T GOT THE HANG OF IT YET!

ANYONE GOT A LADDER?

Answers on pages 118

BET YOU NEVER KNEW!

In the 1990s a Hungarian couple bought a cute white puppy. They became a bit worried when their pet grew very big and smashed up their home. And they were even more alarmed to discover their puppy was really a polar bear!

GRRR!

ER... WALKIES?

A RATHER-TOO-LATE WARNING FROM THE AUTHOR

Baby bears are dangerous. They're strong enough to hurt people and trash your home, and you shouldn't have one as a pet. It's lucky you didn't take our Bear Care Guide too seriously! Oh you did? And you're sending me the bill? Gulp – I'm off to hide in Peru!

But if baby bears can do dreadful things to your furniture, just think what an adult bear could do to YOU! I mean, look at what happened to poor old Hugh Glass. In 1823 Hugh was part of an expedition exploring the wilds of North America…

My Diary by Hugh Glass

August 1823

I'm in a mess. I'm covered in scratches and my leg is broken. I guess it was my fault. I should never have gone into the forest by myself. I never meant to go disturb that mother bear, but she thought I was hunting her cub and attacked me. I had to kill her – but she darn near killed me first...

One week later

← J.B.
J.F. →

All the others have gone but John Fitzgerald and Jim Bridger were left behind to look after me ... until I die. I heard them last night. John was whispering that I was a goner and all they had to do was sneak off and say I was already dead.

One day later...

When I woke up this morning, John and Jim were gone. They've taken all my belongings.
"Grr – I ain't finished yet!" I told myself angrily. So I put a splint on my broken leg and wrapped myself in the bear's skin. My wounds were so rotten I had to roll in maggots.
The hungry little varmints ate the bad bits off me. Then I began to crawl. I'm heading for Fort Kiowa – but it's 320 kilometres. Will I make it?

CHOMP!

GASP!

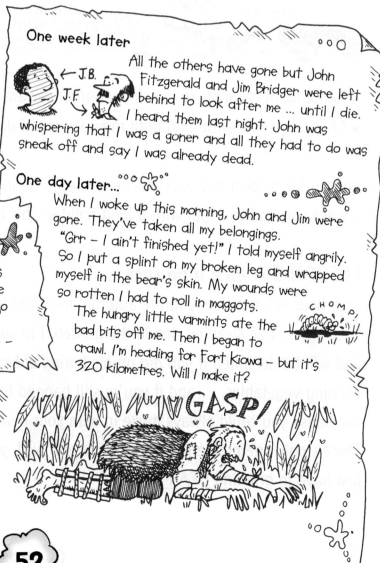

Eight weeks later...
I'm STARVING. I've been living off rotten dead buffalo and berries and snakes, but I won't give up. Some days the pain drives me crazy. If I ever find that John and Jim I'LL KILL THE PAIR OF THEM! That's if I live that long! I've just reached the Cheyenne River and I've just about reached the end of my tether... What now???

One month later...
I owe my life to a tree! I was lying down to die when I saw the tree trunk lying on the riverbank. With the last of my strength I rolled it into the river. Then I floated on the tree down the river to the fort. I was saved.
Now to get even with John and Jim!

You'll be pleased to hear that when Hugh Glass caught up with John and Jim he forgave them. In fact Hugh was lucky. Lucky to find his way to safety and even more lucky to survive the bear's attack. A bear can kill a human with a blow of its paw – it all takes less than 30 seconds.

COULD YOU BE A SCIENTIST?

In 1984 US scientist Doug Dunbar sprayed a new anti-bear pepper spray in a bear's face. What happened?

a) The angry animal chewed up the scientist.

b) Nothing. The bear simply walked away.

c) The angry animal sneezed gloopy bear-snot all over the scientist.

ACHOO!

UGH! IT'S YOGI, I MEAN, **BOGEY** BEAR!

ANSWER:
a) Mind you, it took a few tries before the scientist made a bear angry enough to attack and test the spray. Before then the bears wandered off, so there's half a point for b.

So, bears are quite hard to annoy, it seems. That's interesting. Could it be that bear attacks aren't always the bear's fault? Could humans be to blame?

CONSIDER THESE FACTS:

Rangers in Yellowstone Park, USA, once stopped a woman dabbing honey on her child's face so a bear could lick it off. Another man put a bear in his car to take a photo of it sitting next to his wife. So who was more brainless – the humans or the bears? We've asked a brainy bear to explain the bear's point of view to a rather brainless human...

So maybe bears aren't so cruel?

BEARS BEWARE! QUIZ

North American bears are ferocious. The black bear grows three times heavier than a man ... and then there's the really **BIG** bears. A grizzly bear once bit an Alaskan hunter's head in half and that's after the bear had been shot through the heart. It must have been a grizzly sight. Here's a list of bear safety instructions. All you have to do is sort them into DO'S and DON'TS. See page 118 for the answers.

Bear safety instructions:

1 Go into the forest after a bad berry harvest.

FOUND ANY YET?

NOT ONE!

2 Bandage up any scratches.

3 Shout and make a lot of noise.

SCREAM! CLANG!

TREMBLE SHAKE!

6 Slowly back away.

4 Carry lots of chocolate bars to offer the bears.

5 Eat lots of hamburgers.

7 Stare the bear out to un-nerve it.

8 Lie down and pretend to be dead.

9 Climb a tree.

10 Get between a mother bear and its young.

CRUEL BIG CATS

Please answer the following questions...
1 Do you live with a cat?
2 Does your cat enjoy playing with half-dead mice,
staring hungrily at the budgie and sinking her claws into the postman?

GULP!

If you answered "yes" to both of the above questions it's quite likely that you own a cruel cat. But even the cruellest cat is a cutesy-pie kitten compared to this lot... No wonder they didn't want the cat food.

Angry animals fact file

NAME OF CREATURE:
Tiger and lion (joint entry) – we're looking at both animals because they both kill lots of people.

TYPE OF ANIMAL: Mammal

DIET: Meat, meat and more meat – ideally large four-footed creatures. Lions like wildebeest and zebra. Tigers eat several species of Indian deer. Oh yes, and neither species minds munching a human...

NUMBER OF PEOPLE KILLED: Each year lions kill hundreds of people in Africa and tigers kill over 100 people in India.

WHERE THEY LIVE: Lions live on open plains in Africa (with a few in India). Tigers live in forests, mainly in India and Nepal with a few in South-east Asia, China and Russia.

SIZE: Lions and tigers grow up to 2.7 metres long including their tails.

FEARSOME FEATURES:

LION

Paws the size of a man's head.

Greasy waterproof coat.

Canine teeth for biting prey.

Claws as thick as a man's thumb for pulling down prey.

Flesh-slicing back teeth.

GRRR!

TIGER

Slightly bulging eyes for all-round vision.

Stripy coat to blend in with long grass and forest.

Soft paws for silent creeping.

Ruthless relatives

Although lions and tigers look different, they're part of the same group of animals – scientists call them the Panthera, or roaring cats. (Your cat isn't a roaring cat – she's a mewing cat. Especially when she wants more supper and she's trying to make you feel sorry for her.) But here's some roaring panthera you really wouldn't want to meet on a dark night...

JAGUAR

Size: Up to 1.9 metres long.

Lives: Forests in South America.

Danger-rating: Rarely attacks humans but does enjoy sinking its fangs into a victim's brain. Maybe it's hungry for knowledge...

PUMA

(alias the cougar or mountain lion and I bet if one attacked you, you might like to call it other names).

Size: Up to 2.4 metres long.

Lives: Wild parts of North and South America.

Danger-rating: Can attack people but deaths are very rare.

LEOPARD

Size: Up to 2.5 metres long (including tail).

Lives: Plains in Africa and forests in India.

Danger-rating: They normally hunt monkeys and antelopes but they have a horribly antisocial habit of breaking into huts and grabbing people in their sleep. And a leopard can knock the spots off a human in a fight.

As you've just found out lions and tigers live in different places,
but let's imagine a lion cub and tiger cub met for a chat.
OK, I realize this is going to take a bit of imagining...

Tiger cub   HELLO!   Lion cub   HI!

TC: Mum feeds me.

LC: Mum and Gran and Mum's sisters feed me. We're called a pride – well, Mum's proud of us!

TC: We only feed every few days.

LC: So do we – blimey I'm starving!

TC: Mum lets me eat first.

LC: Huh – you're lucky! I have to eat last.

TC: I never see my dad.

LC: My dad rules the pride.

TC: My mum made a chemical message in her wee to attract my dad.

LC: So did my mum. Grown-ups are s-o-o disgusting!

TC: My dad makes a Aoooom! sound to warn off other tigers.

LC: My dad roars.

TC: If a new male tiger takes over my dad's territory he could kill me.

LC: If a new male takes over the pride he could kill me.

WE HAVE IT TOUGH!

TC: Fancy a game of chase?

LC: OK – you're IT!

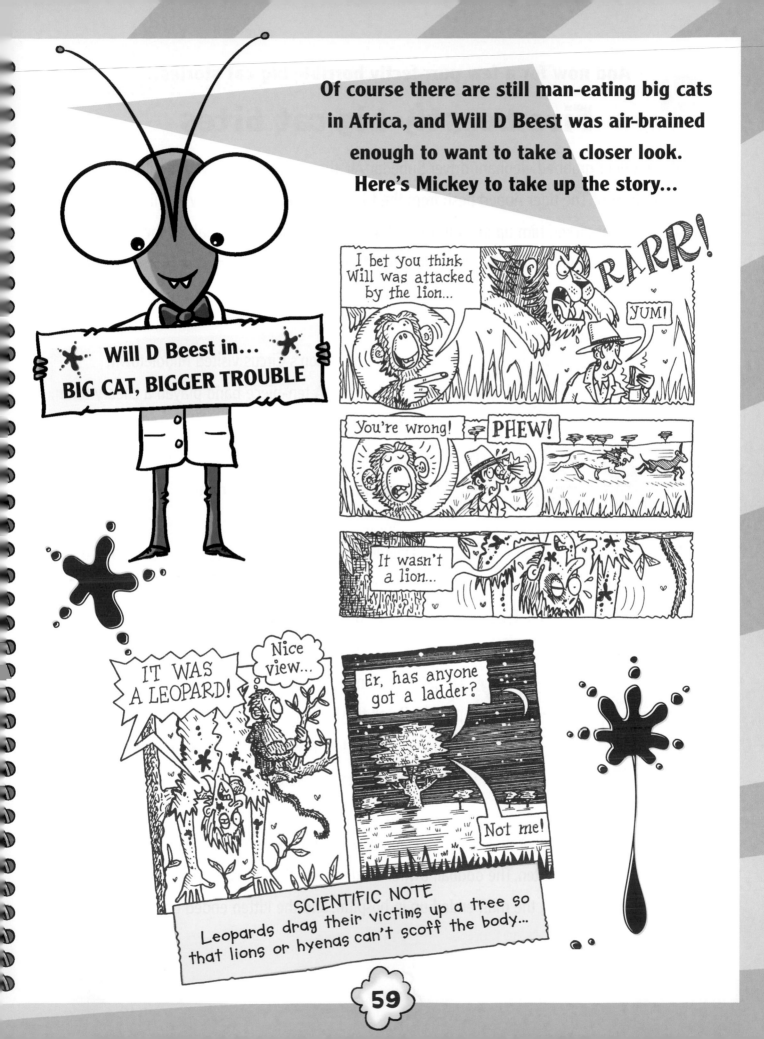

Five beastly big cat bites

1 When a tiger grabbed elephant driver Subedar Ali, the young man prayed to all the gods he could think of. The tiger ripped flesh from the top of Ali's head and nearly bit his fingers off. But Ali's elephant picked him up in its trunk and pulled him to safety. Officials at the Corbett National Park, India, wanted to shoot the tiger but Ali begged for the animal to be saved. His wish was granted. The tiger was sent to a zoo and Subedar Ali visited it to say "hello".

DROP IN ANYTIME!

2 In 1870 James Robinson's Circus visited Middletown, Missouri, in the USA. A ten-piece band played a cheery tune on top of the lions' cage. But the roof was weak. With a bang and a crash the band fell into the lions' cage and seven of them were eaten. So I guess the lions got a taste for music…

3 In 1937 an English vicar called Harold Davidson was sitting in a cage with a lion named Freddie. (The vicar was trying to make some money after losing his job.) But when the clumsy cleric trod on his tail, Freddie began to feast on the priest with fatal results.

EATEN B-B-B-Y MY
OWN R-R-RELATIVE…
F-F-F-F-FREAKY!

4 Despite the danger, thousands of people keep big cats as pets. In Brazil they're kept as guard dogs – er, cats – and burglars have been eaten. (I wonder if they were beefy burglars, cheesy burglars or even veggie burglars.)

5 In 2003 a man in New York kept a tiger, an alligator and a kitten as pets. But the tiger decided to eat the kitten. The oddball owner tried to save the kitten and got bitten. The big animals ended up in zoos, the man ended up in hospital, and the kitten ended up in shock.

PROWLERS ON THE PLAIN

Some animals are cute and cuddly but the animals in this book aren't like that. They're angry animals that sometimes attack humans. We've hired visiting aliens Oddblob the Blurb and Slobslime the Snottie to find out more about these killer creatures. They're in for a really beastly trip...

HO RIBLE HUNTE S

When you're hungry you probably pop out to the shops to buy food. It's called "shopping". Animals can't usually do this so, instead, they pop out and nab some unfortunate, small creature for their tea. Here's how they do it.

Horrible hunter types

Some hunters, such as lions and tigers, eat large animals. For them life is rather relaxing. They spend most of their life sleeping off huge meals. They only hunt when they're really hungry. It helps to keep out of their way at these times. Other hunters such as wild dogs or hyenas will eat anything that comes along and they're always on the look out for a free lunch. Best avoid them at all times.

AND BEWARE. Hunters play horrible tricks.

Horrible hunter tricks

THEY HAVEN'T TWIGGED YET

1 Sneak up on your victim. If they turn round freeze and pretend to be a twig. The olive green snake of Central America does this. It even sways in the breeze – before it strikes and grabs a poor little baby bird from its nest.

2 The horned frog sits motionless except for one finger. This twitches until an insect or small creature comes by thinking it's something to eat. Big mistake. It's feeding time all right – feeding time for the frog.

3 There's a type of African mongoose with a bottom that looks like a small flower. The mongoose crouches on a shrub with its bum in the air. When an insect lands on the pretty "flower" the mongoose whips round and snaps it up.

4 White-coated polar bears are almost invisible against the Arctic snow. But the bear's large black nose is embarrassingly obvious when it sneaks up on a seal. So the bears push a lump of ice in front of them to hide their tell-tale noses.

5 Everyone knows that rattlesnakes have a rattle at the end of their tails. Some of their few fans say that the rattle is there to warn people to steer clear. Huh – as if snakes are that thoughtful. In fact, the rattle is there to attract attention away from the head with its fatal fangs.

Could you be as cunning as these horrible hunters? Now's your chance to find out. Imagine you were a lioness living on the plains of Southern Africa. What sort of a hunter would you make?

Lion hunting tips

The lionesses in a pride (group of lions) hunt together.
(The lazy males don't take part.)

1 **Your pride of lionesses stalks a herd of gazelles (small antelope). From what direction do you approach?**

a) With the wind at your back so that the gazelles can smell you. This will scare them so much they won't be able to defend themselves.

b) With the wind blowing in your face so the gazelles can't smell you.

c) From the direction of the sun so that the gazelles are dazzled.

2 **Your pride splits into two groups. What do you do next?**

a) One group charges the gazelles and chases them towards the second group waiting in ambush.

b) One group goes after the gazelles and the others chase some nearby zebra. This doubles the chance of catching something.

c) One group chases gazelles and the others keep watch for marauding hyenas that might try to steal the meat.

3 **You select a gazelle to attack. Which one do you choose?**

a) The biggest – more meat for you.

b) The smallest – less likely to put up a fight.

c) The weakest – easier to catch.

4 **The males invite themselves to the feast. While you and your sisters have been hunting the males have been lazing about in the sun. Now they're hungry. So who gets the lion's share?**

a) The lionesses, followed by the cubs. The males are given a few scraps. Serves 'em right for not helping.

b) The males take the best bits. The lionesses and the cubs get what's left. If they're lucky.

c) The cubs. After all they need the food to help them grow.

WHAT'S FOR PUDDING, MUM?

5 **A new male chases away the old males in your pride. He cruelly kills and eats your cubs. What do you do?**

a) Run for the hills.

b) Kill him and eat his body.

c) Make friends with him.

6 **In the dry season there's little food. What do you eat?**

a) Other lions

b) Fish, insects, lizards, mice and the odd tortoise.

c) Bones buried for just such an emergency.

See page 118 for the answers

What your score means:

5–6 A roar of approval. You'd make a great hunter.

3–4 You're mane-ly right but you need to lick your skills into shape.

1–2 You'll never be a lion. Best swallow your "pride" and stick to being a human.

One of the fiercest hunters is one that you may have met already. Indeed this ferocious creature may be lurking behind your curtains or even watching your TV! Yes – we're talking about your not-so-cuddly cat. Here's where we let the cat out of the bag. Your pet leads a deadly double-life.

Tiddles the terrible

Tiddles rubs your legs. Just trying to be friendly? No way. She's leaving her scent on you to show you're part of HER family.

THAT'S MY GIRL

BOUNDARY LINE

GET LOST!

Tiddles has her own hunting territory. Normally she won't allow any other cat into this area. The territory is a little larger than your garden.

FREEZE POSITION   POUNCE POSTURE

Tiddles hunts by sneaking up on prey. Sometimes she freezes before moving stealthily forward once more. At the last moment she pounces.

Tiddles enjoys catching insects. They have such a lovely crunchy texture – it's just like you eating crisps.

BIZZ BUZZ

But she doesn't like catching rabbits or rats.
She's scared of rabbits because they're so big. And she thinks that
rats taste worse than cheap cat food.

When Tiddles "plays" with mice she's not being cruel. Oh no?
She's just a big scaredy-cat. Scared the mouse will fight back (some mice do).
So she keeps her distance without losing the mouse.

Tiddles eats mice head first. Gulp.
Before eating birds she plucks out the feathers with her teeth.

When Tiddles brings you a half-dead mouse or battered bird
it's her way of teaching you to hunt. Yes – she wants you to finish it off.
Mother cats do this to train their kittens.

STUNNING SENSE STATS

IT'S OFFICIAL – animals are sensitive. But even if they didn't have feelings, they'd still be sensitive because animals have some pretty incredible senses. Which they need to survive in their favourite habitats. But how do they measure up to humans? Surely they couldn't compete?

STUNNING SENSE STATISTICS

ANIMAL SENSES 	HUMAN SENSES
SUPERSNIFFERS When you walk about in bare feet you leave 4 billionths of a gram of sweat in each footprint. To a dog this stinks like a cheesy old pair of socks that haven't been washed for a month.	**DON'T SMELL TOO WELL** A human's sense of smell is one million times weaker than a dog's.  EVEN THOUGH HIS NOSE IS TWICE AS BIG
EAGLE EYES A golden eagle can see a rabbit on the ground up to 3.2 km away.	**A SIGHT FOR SORE EYES** Some humans trip over rabbits.
A NASTY TASTE IN THE MOUTH Ugly catfish that lurk at the bottom of South American rivers have well over 250,000 taste buds in their tongues. That's how they find food in the murky mud.	**TOTALLY TASTELESS** Humans only have 10,000 taste buds – that's half as many as a pig. (This may explain why pigs don't enjoy school dinners but some humans do.)
HEAR, HERE 1. A dog's ear has at least 18 muscles so it can turn in any direction. 2. The Californian leaf-nosed bat can hear the footsteps of insects.	**HARD OF HEARING HUMANS** 1. Humans only have nine ear muscles and most people can't even waggle theirs. 2. Can you? NO!

A TOUCH OF MAGIC

Seals use their ultra-sensitive whiskers to pick up tiny movements in the water caused by another creature.

A TOUCHY SUBJECT

Human whiskers don't even twitch.

IT'S TRUE!

STRANGE SENSES

1. Animals can predict earthquakes. In 2003 Japanese scientists found that mice behave oddly when they detect changes in magnetic forces linked to quakes.

2. The American knife-fish produces an electric signal 300 times every second. This creates a force field around the animal. A disturbance in the field warns the fish there's another creature about.

SENSELESS

1. Weedy humans can't accurately predict earthquakes even using sophisticated scientific instruments.

2. Er . . .

OK, YOU WIN!

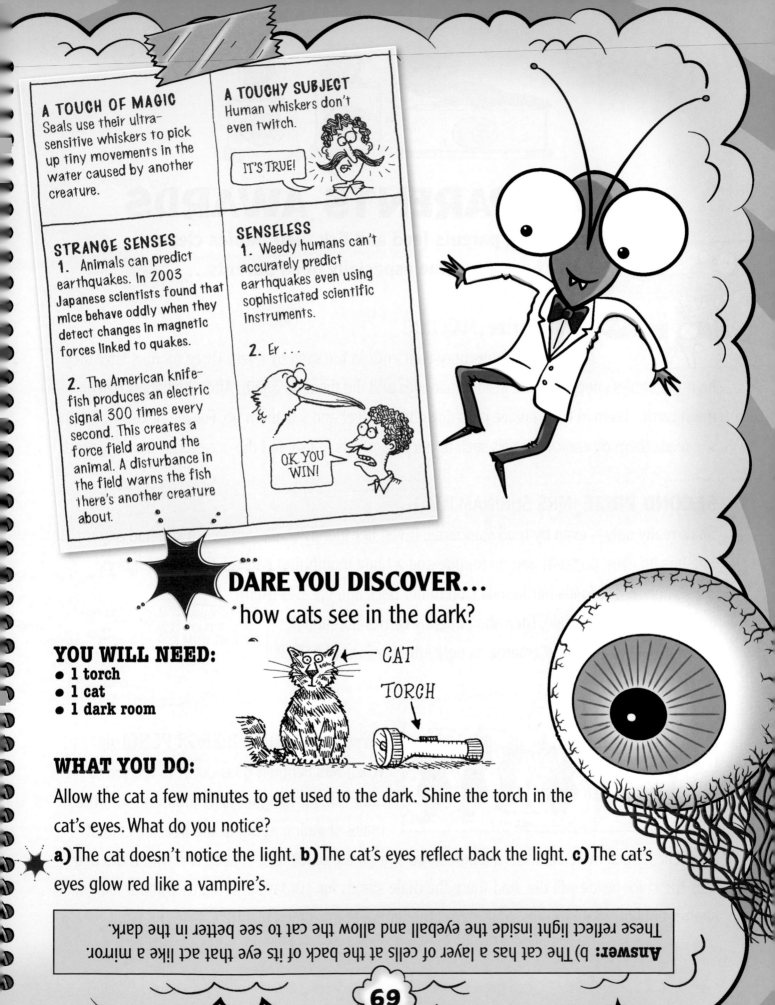

DARE YOU DISCOVER...

how cats see in the dark?

YOU WILL NEED:
- 1 torch
- 1 cat
- 1 dark room

CAT

TORCH

WHAT YOU DO:

Allow the cat a few minutes to get used to the dark. Shine the torch in the cat's eyes. What do you notice?

a) The cat doesn't notice the light. b) The cat's eyes reflect back the light. c) The cat's eyes glow red like a vampire's.

Answer: b) The cat has a layer of cells at the back of its eye that act like a mirror. These reflect light inside the eyeball and allow the cat to see better in the dark.

GOOD PARENTS AWARDS

**Many animal parents feed and lick their babies clean.
And here are some especially good parents...**

Third prize MA CROC

Crocodile mums bury their eggs in the sand by rivers. Three months later they hear the babies cheeping from inside their eggs and dig them up again. After the babies hatch, mum carries them in her massive jaws down to the river and lets them go. For the next few months she feeds them on choice morsels such as juicy frogs, bits of fish and the occasional crunchy insect.

SECOND PRIZE MRS SURINAM TOAD

She's really ugly – even by toad standards. (Even her friends would agree – if she had any.) She has no eyes, no teeth and no tongue and a huge mouth that eats anything that moves. Yet somehow she loads her tadpoles on to her back and encases them in bubbles under her skin. Then she patiently carries the tadpoles for two months until they emerge as ugly little versions of herself.

WE'RE GOING OUT TO PLAY FOR A BIT, MUM

I GIVE UP – ANYONE FANCY A GAME OF FOOTBALL?

DISGRACEFUL!

First prize MR EMPEROR PENGUIN

When Mrs Penguin goes down to the sea to hunt fish, Mr Penguin joins thousands of other males standing about in the freezing cold of Antarctica. Each male balances a single large egg on top of his feet to keep it warm. If the egg falls the chick inside will die. And there the male stands for 40 days and nights without food or shelter until his mate returns. Sometimes the temperatures drops to -40°C (-40°F). What a hero!

Lethal lessons

If you're a baby animal you need to learn some urgent lessons in survival. And if you're lucky your parents will teach you.

1 **Guillemot chicks** have to learn how to swim and fly. So their parents chuck them off a cliff. If they fly – good. If not, they'd better learn to swim.

2 **Mother swallows** take food to their chicks but hover just out of reach. If the chicks want to grab their grub they'd better learn to fly first.

3 **Cheetah mums** catch a gazelle and then release it for their cubs to chase. If the gazelle escapes the cubs get taught a lesson: they starve.

4 Eventually, when her cubs get too big, a **grizzly bear mum** chases them up a tree and wanders off. Now begins the biggest lesson of all: how to survive alone.

PIGEON POWER

Now you might think a pigeon is a silly-looking bird with a tiny little head and a puny little brain to match. And of course, you'd be right. But when it comes to travelling, pigeons and many other birds are geographical geniuses.

INCREDIBLE EYESIGHT

DIRECTION-FINDING BRAIN

SUPERSONIC HEARING

AMAZING FLYING POWERS

BIG FAT FLUFFY CHEST

1 Pigeons can fly all day at speeds of 48 km per hour (30 mph) and cover 1,120 km and still not get tired.

2 Pigeons' brains contain magnetic crystals sensitive to the Earth's magnetic field. This allows a pigeon to know which direction is north and which direction is home. This was proved in the 1970s when a scientist tied a magnet to a pigeon's head. The magnet confused the pigeon's crystals and the poor pigeon got lost.

3 Like other birds that fly long distances, pigeons can recognize landmarks and use the position of the sun and the stars to work out directions. They can even see rays of sunlight when the sun is behind a cloud.

4 And if all that wasn't enough, pigeons have the ability to hear ultra low-pitched sounds too low for a human ear. For example, a pigeon can hear waves crashing on a beach hundreds of kilometres away. That's how they know the way to the seaside.

5 With all these amazing abilities you won't be surprised to hear that a homing pigeon that wins races is worth its weight in gold. One such bird, Emerald, was sold in 1988 for £77,000 and even her eggs were worth £2,400 each. Drop a few of those and you could make the world's most expensive omelette.

DOES ANYONE KNOW WHAT HAPPENED TO THE EGGS THAT "EMERALD" LAID YESTERDAY?

But pigeons are just one species of high-flying, long-distance-travelling birds. Lots of birds migrate or travel from one area to another – every year. They do this because they have a powerful urge to fly off in a certain direction to find more food or a suitable nesting site. But scientists don't really understand how and why the birds manage it. Would you enjoy a holiday like this?

WiNG~iT HoLiDAYS

SWIFT TOURS

Air tours of sunny south-east Africa. Get away from the nasty British winter. Non-stop air flights with in-flight refreshments. Just catch yourself a few crunchy insects on the way. Exclusive washing facilities – just whiz through a thunderstorm. Note to passengers: the trip covers 19,200 km and we won't be landing at all. Not even to visit the toilet.

WANDERING ALBATROSS TOURS

Antarctica is the last unspoilt continent on Earth. Now you can fly around its beautiful coast in search of fish. Enjoy panoramic views and a lovely smooth ride. Your wandering albatross pilot can glide for six days without beating a wing. In-flight meals include mouth-watering raw fish – with that "just caught" taste.

ARCTIC TERN TOURS

A holiday with a difference. Good weather is guaranteed! Yes, you can be sure that every day will "tern" out nice again! Escape the northern winter blues by flying direct to sunny Antarctica where the days are warmest at this time of year. Then back to the Arctic in time for summer. Lovely fish suppers are available all the way too.

DON'T GET IN A FLAP!

Grab your pencil and have a go at drawing this bird-brained bunch.

UGLY BUGS

Now it's time to think small, horribly small. There are many times more types of insects than all other animals put together and there are probably far more types of microbes than insects... See page 119 for the answers.

Incredible bug discoveries quiz

Here are five places that new bugs or microbes have been found – the only problem is that TWO of these places are made up. Which are made up and which are true?

a) Lake Vostock: an underground lake deep beneath the snows of Antarctica.

b) The mouth of a lobster.

c) Deep within an active volcano in Switzerland.

d) On the body of a wasp.

e) Inside the glowing bulb of a sodium street light.

YIKES, I HOPE IT'S NOT b)!

Ugly bug true and false quiz

This is a straightforward quiz – you just say TRUE or FALSE to each question. But there's an ugly twist: for each wrong answer you LOSE a point. For this reason you need someone to read you the quiz and keep note of your score!

1 A magathon is a maggot race organized by the World Organization of Racing Maggots (WORM) at Barney's Bar in Montana, USA. TRUE or FALSE?

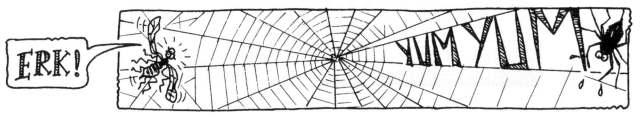

THAT'S ONLY HALF A MAGGOT – WHERE D'YOU FIND IT?

IN THAT APPLE YOU ATE AT LUNCHTIME

2 Insects have been found living on Mars (that's the planet not the chocolate bars). TRUE or FALSE?

3 Blow flies can taste food through their feet. TRUE or FALSE?

4 Mind you, that's nothing – an ichneumon (ick-noy-mon) fly can hear and smell through its feet. TRUE or FALSE?

YOU'LL HAVE TO SPEAK UP. I'VE GOT MY SHOES ON.

5 The chocolate beetle only eats chocolate. It sneaks into houses and can scoff a whole bar by itself. TRUE or FALSE?

6 Tarantula spiders fire tiny spears at mice. TRUE or FALSE?

7 The sea cucumber is a kind of sea slug that defends itself by squirting its guts over an attacker. TRUE or FALSE?

8 Felicity Whitman of Arizona, USA, has taught spiders to spell words in their webs and ants to nibble patterns in lettuce leaves. TRUE or FALSE?

ERK!

YUM YUM

Mantids and cockroaches

At least 6,500 species. There's a strong family resemblance in their horrible habits. Cockroaches make midnight raids on the pantry. The praying mantis sits around cunningly disguised as part of a plant, and waits to pounce on its innocent victims.

WHAT A BEAUTIFUL PLANT

IT'S ME, YOU STUPID COCKROACH!

Bugs

Over 100,000 species in this order worldwide. They suck vegetable juices through straw-like mouths. Nothing ugly about that, you might think, except some do like a bit of blood now and then.

Flies

Far more than 120,000 species in this order. They use one pair of wings for flying (which is what they do best). They also have the remnants of a second pair of wings that look like tiny drumsticks, and are actually used for balancing. Most irritating fly habit: flying backwards, sideways and forwards round your head. OK – so you know they're incredible fliers already. Nastiest fly habit: some types of fly like nothing better than to lick the top of a big smelly cowpat. And then pay a visit to whatever you were going to have for tea.

Sucking lice

More than 500 species. Lice don't build their own homes. No. They live on other creatures. It's nice and warm there and you can suck a refreshing drop of blood whenever you feel like it. Lice can live on nearly every mammal – bats are one of the few exceptions. Or at least no one has ever found a louse on a bat.

Dragonflies, caddis flies, mayflies

...are three different orders totalling more than 17,000 species. They start off living in water and then take to the air. Traditional names for dragonflies include "horse stingers" and "devil's darning needles". Which is odd because they don't sting horses and you can't mend your socks with them.

MAYFLY   CADDIS FLY   DRAGONFLY

I DON'T LOOK LIKE A DRAGON EITHER!

Butterflies and moths

Well over 180,000 species in this order worldwide. They have two pairs of wings and their young start off as caterpillars. Then they hide in a case called a chrysalis and re-arrange their body parts before emerging as butterflies or moths. It's a bit like you spending a few weeks taking your body apart in a sleeping bag. And then putting it all back together in a different order.

So these are the ugly insects, but what about their even more repulsive relatives?

Nasty non-insects

If an ugly bug has got more than six legs – or no legs at all, it isn't an insect.

Slugs and snails

Over 35,000 species on land and many live in the sea. Slimy slugs and snails belong to a huge group of animals called the molluscs that even includes octopuses. But slugs and snails are the only members of the group that have tentacles on their heads.

Centipedes and millipedes

...are two different classes of ugly bugs. There are about 2,800 species of centipede and more than 10,000 species of millipede. But sinister centipedes gobble up the poor little millipedes and not the other way round.

MILLIPEDE (A WORRIED ONE)

CENTIPEDE (A HUNGRY ONE)

Woodlice

Over 3,500 species. They all have seven pairs of legs. Woodlice, would you believe it, belong to the same class of creature as crabs and lobsters!

Spiders

There are 37,000 species in this order but scientists think there may be up to five times that number waiting to be discovered! What a thought! Most spiders spin silken webs. They have eight legs, of course, and their bodies are divided into two parts.

WHEEEEE!

CRIKEY – BUNGEE JUMPING!

MONEY SPIDER

TARANTULA SPIDER

Earthworms, bristleworms and leeches

More than 16,000 species altogether. Leeches are the nasty bloodsuckers. When a leech sucks blood it can swell up to three times its original size. There are 300 different leech species. Yuck! One is enough!

Mites

There are well over 45,000 species in this order. Unlike spiders, mites have a one-piece body. Many mites are under 1 mm long but they still have some hugely horrible habits. Some eat cheese rinds and the glue in old books. Others suck blood from animals.

MUNCH MUNCH

THIS IS A GOOD BOOK, WE'RE GLUED TO IT!

A MITE

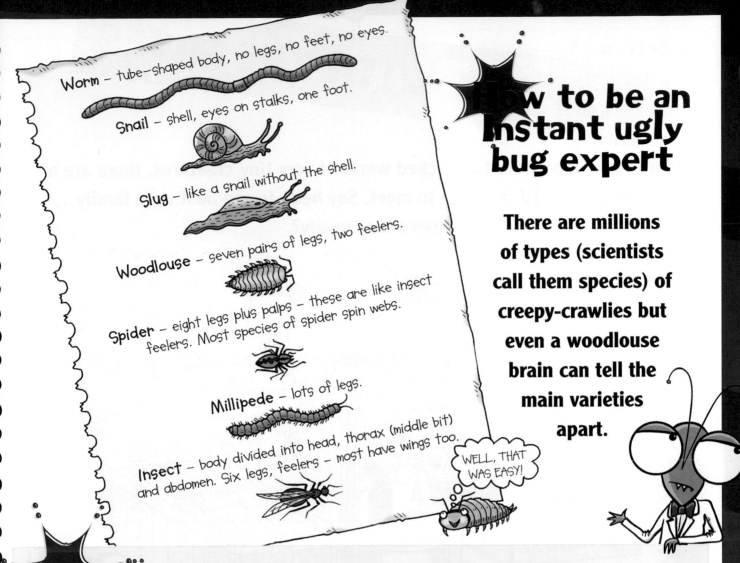

Worm – tube-shaped body, no legs, no feet, no eyes.

Snail – shell, eyes on stalks, one foot.

Slug – like a snail without the shell.

Woodlouse – seven pairs of legs, two feelers.

Spider – eight legs plus palps – these are like insect feelers. Most species of spider spin webs.

Millipede – lots of legs.

Insect – body divided into head, thorax (middle bit) and abdomen. Six legs, feelers – most have wings too.

WELL, THAT WAS EASY!

How to be an instant ugly bug expert

There are millions of types (scientists call them species) of creepy-crawlies but even a woodlouse brain can tell the main varieties apart.

DARE YOU DISCOVER... How to walk like a millipede

Like worms, woodlice and centipedes, millipede bodies are divided into segments. Each segment has two pairs of legs, but how on earth do they manage to walk without tripping over?

YOU WILL NEED:
● Yourself (It helps if all your arms and legs are firmly attached – I'd hate to think of them dropping off during the experiment.)

WHAT YOU DO:
1. Crouch on your hands and knees.
2. Move your right and left hands forward one step.
3. Move both your knees forward one step.

Shuffle! Slide!

YOU SHOULD FIND: Congratulations you've moved one segment of your millipede body! Now imagine doing all this over and over again to move your 746 other legs…

AT HOME WITH THE MITES

Before we escape from the wicked world of very tiny creatures, there are a few little friends I'd love you to meet. Say hello to the dust mite family... Aren't they lovely?

grasping claws   8 "hairy" legs   body armour

WHAT'S FOR PUDDING?

NIBBLE!   MUNCH!

SKIN CRUMBLE.

BABY MITE   PA MITE   MA MITE   0.44 mm long

Yes that's right, they eat dead skin (your rotting flesh). And what's more THEY LIVE IN YOUR BED!

The half a house of horror
We've cut this nice family home in half with a huge chainsaw to show your mite mates' hideaways...

YIKES, WHERE'S THE WALL?!

BRR — IT'S SUDDENLY GOT CHILLY!

MITE MY HOUSE

HOW ARE YOU, MITE?

Red spider mites wander in from the garden.

Conure parrots have 30 types of mite living in their feathers.

I THOUGHT YOU MITE DROP BY!

MITE CAFE

OOER!

MITE ZOO

MUNCH!

Flour mites munch leftover food.

PASS THE DRIBBLE.

DON'T PANIC! You've been sleeping with mites all your life and they've never done any harm (probably). So sleep tight and be glad the mites don't bite. Not like the brutal bloodthirsty bugs in the next section…

SLIMY SNAILS AND UGLY SLUGS

They're covered in slime, slide along very slowly and have eyes on the end of stalks. And if that's not ugly enough, they gobble up your garden lettuce. So it's not surprising that people don't like them. But are slugs and snails really that horrible? Do they deserve their rotten reputation? Yes they do. And here's why.

Ugly bug fact file

NAME OF CREATURE: Slugs and snails

WHERE THEY LIVE: Worldwide in the soil, in the sea and in fresh water. Land slugs and snails like damp places.

DISTINGUISIHING FEATURES: Snails have shells on their backs. Slugs don't.

SHELL   GHASTLY SLIMY ANTENNAE

BREATHING HOLE

FOOT   HEAD

REVOLTING SLIMY BODY   FOOT

BET YOU NEVER KNEW!
An ugly slug can tell you which way the wind is blowing.
It's true. A slug will always crawl away from the prevailing wind.
Slugs do this to stop themselves drying out too quickly

Seven slimy snail facts you didn't really want to know

1 The largest snail in the world is the African Giant snail. It can be 34 cm from its shell top to its head! It eats bananas – and dead animals.

2 The garlic grass snail smells strongly of garlic. OK – it's not really horrible. But it must give snail-eating birds horribly bad breath.

3 When a snail is chomping away on your mum's prize cauliflowers, it will be using its radula – that's its tongue. The radula is so rough it actually grates its food.

THEY WERE TASTY – BUT I'VE NO ONE TO PLAY WITH NOW!

4 The slimiest sea snails are dog whelks. They lay their eggs in a tough capsule attached to the sea bed. But some of the youngsters seize and guzzle their own brothers and sisters as soon as they hatch out!

5 Some sea snails on the other hand, eat meat. These snails have a few sharp teeth – well suited for catching and chomping on their prey!

6 Another slimy sea snail is the oyster drill. Here's how an oyster drill drills:

a) It makes a chemical that softens up the oyster shell.

b) It scrapes the shell with its radula, repeating step a) as required.

c) It sticks its feeding tube through the hole and slurps up the juicy oyster!

7 But snails don't have it all their own way. A tiny worm lives inside the amber snail. Sometimes the worm releases chemicals that turn the snail's tentacles orange! This colourful display attracts a bird that nips off the snail's crowning glory. The worm begins a whole gruesome new life inside the bird. And the snail? It grows new tentacles. So that's all right then.

Ugly slugs

A slug is just a snail without a mobile home on its back. Come to think of it, slugs have the right idea. Have you ever seen a snail trying to get under a low bridge? Not having a shell helps slugs slither into nooks and crannies. But slugs have some scintillating secrets. That's if you dare discover them.

DARE YOU... make friends with an ugly slug?

Here's how to snuggle up to a slug. Who knows, you could be in for a horribly interesting encounter!

1 First meet your slug. You can tell where there are slugs around by the horrible silvery slime trails they leave. They like to slither about in the open on warm damp summer evenings. So just follow a tempting trail until you find your slug lurking under the leaves of a small plant.

2 Enjoy that gooey, squelchy feeling between your fingers as you put your slug in a glass jar.

SQUELCH

3 Watch in amazement as your ugly slug climbs the slippery walls of the jar. It moves on a layer of slime produced by its foot. The sticky slime allows the slug to cling to the glass. Waves of movement push its foot forward. Think about it – could you climb up a glass wall on just one foot that's been dipped in something rather like raw egg?

4 Imagine you were a bird. Would you want to eat the slug? Not likely – the slime tastes disgusting! But hedgehogs think they are horribly delicious.

5 Put your new friend back where you found him/her. That way you'll stay friends.

IF YOU GO SLUG HUNTING in your garden on a warm damp night you might meet a shield-shelled slug. (Try saying that very fast – three times!) This sinister slug gets its name from a tiny shell on the top end of its body. But can you guess what it eats? CLUE: It isn't lettuce.

Answer: Earthworms, centipedes and other slugs. Delicious!

Seven ugly slug facts

1 The largest British ugly slug is the great grey slug. It grows to 20 cm long!

SEA SLUG

REVOLTING FLESHY PROJECTIONS

2 But that's nothing! Some sea slugs are 40 cm long and weigh 7 kilos. They are also often brightly coloured.

♪ A LIFE ON THE OCEAN WAVE... ♪

3 And some of them have some horribly strange habits. Glaucus is a sea slug that floats upside down buoyed up by an air bubble inside its stomach.

4 Meanwhile back on the farm, slugs and farmers are sworn enemies because ugly slugs eat or spoil crops. If slugs didn't eat potatoes there would be enough extra chips to feed 400,000 people for a year!

5 Like worms and snails, slugs are both male and female at the same time.

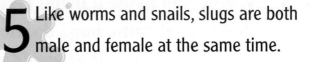

6 When slugs mate they cling together and cover themselves in slime. Then they fire little arrows called love darts at one another to get in the mood. Very romantic – if you're a slug!

7 Land slugs have some horribly strange habits as well. Some ugly slugs can let themselves down from a height on a string of slime.

HELLO MUM!

BU GLAR BUGS

Just imagine you made a living creeping into people's houses and trashing them! That's what some bugs do. Hopefully you haven't got too many of this lot. Now that would add horror to your home!

Cleaning Services

DOES YOUR HOSPITAL NEED A SPRING CLEAN? Pharaoh Ant Cleaning Services will eat your unwanted bloody bandages. We'll even leave a free sample of 19 disease-causing microbes to share with your patients!

UGH! I CAN'T EAT ANY MORE!

PHAROAH-NUFF!

Tired of your old home?

Carpenter Ant Services will get rid of it fast! We'll eat all those ugly old beams holding up your home.

CRUMPH!

NICE ONE!

If your house gets you down we'll bring it down!

MAKE GREASY STAINS A THING OF THE PAST!

The Grease Ants will remove all your grease and any dead rats or mice lying around! It's a free service! Don't be shy — apply today!

Are pests spoiling your life?

Call in Army Ant Pest Control (South America only). All two million of us will march through your living room and eat everything alive! Just make sure you wake granny up and put the cat out!

TOO LATE!

Tired of your damp kitchen?

Time to redecorate with Slug Services! We'll transform your boring old lino with beautiful silvery slime trails! All we ask are a few mouldy lettuce leaves the rabbit didn't want!

BUT I DID WANT THEM!

Old woodwork can be a worry!

YOU NEED TERMITE TIMBER TREATMENT! We'll eat your problem timber. And we'll even eat your non-problem timber! We'll chew through concrete if we have to. Then we'll build a GIGANTIC luxury termite nest where your home used to be!

Luxury air conditioning caused by rising warm air

CHOMP!

NEST FOR SALE

FEELING LONELY?

YOU NEED A PET HOUSE CRICKET! No kennel required – a pile of rotting rubbish will do! Your little pal will keep you company with its cheeky chirping. And it won't stop when you're trying to sleep.

CHIRRRRRUP!

SHUT UP!

KIND-HEARTED FAMILY NEEDED!

It's a cold night. Could you offer a home to a poor little woodlouse family? Simply water your carpet with a watering can or your guests will dry out in the night! PS Please scatter rotting vegetables around your house for them to eat.

MUNCH!

THANKS!

BET YOU NEVER KNEW!

Are your bug guests getting you down? Just hope they don't invite their rotten relatives!

1 Time for a midnight feast. You tiptoe to the fridge and ... SQUISH! Your toes squelch a cold, slimy SLUG! Oh well, at least it's not a ghost slug. This sinister slobbery slitherer lurks in Asian caves. It scoffs bat poo and sucks worms like spaghetti. Luckily it doesn't come into houses and it doesn't gobble toes.

2 A wicked woodlouse relative Cymothoa (simo-tho-a) sneaks into the mouth of spotted rose snapper fish. And eats their tongue. Then it gobbles the food the famished fish is trying to feed on.

YUM YUM!

GRRRRR!

AWESOME ANTS

Everyone knows about ants. They're easy enough to identify in the summer when they march into your home to inspect your kitchen. Ants can be pretty awful – they get everywhere from your plants to your pants – but they can be awesome, too, in all sorts of horrible ways.

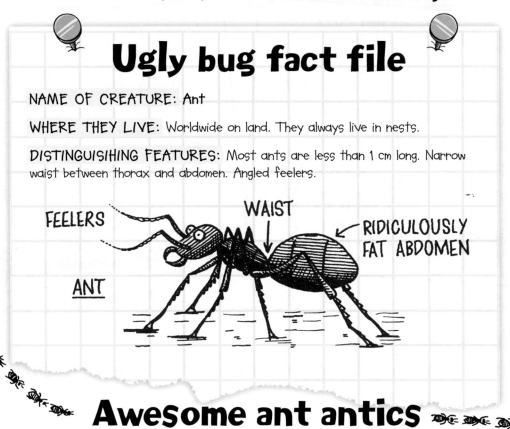

Ugly bug fact file

NAME OF CREATURE: Ant

WHERE THEY LIVE: Worldwide on land. They always live in nests.

DISTINGUISHING FEATURES: Most ants are less than 1 cm long. Narrow waist between thorax and abdomen. Angled feelers.

FEELERS

WAIST

RIDICULOUSLY FAT ABDOMEN

ANT

Awesome ant antics

1 Since 1880 German law has protected red ants' nests from destruction. Why? Because the ants from each nest eat an amazing 100,000 caterpillars and other ugly pests every day.

2 Weaver ants make their own tents from leaves sewn together with silk. Their larvae produce the silk and the awesome ants use their young as living shuttles weaving them backwards and forwards! The adult ants just have to touch their larvae with their feelers whenever they need a bit more silk.

3 Honeypot ants squeeze sticky honeydew from aphids. They're doing the aphids a favour – they don't need the sickly stuff. The ants keep feeding this honeydew to particular

SHE'S GOING TO BE SICK ~ DINNER TIME EVERYONE!

ants in their nest to make them swell up like little beads. The swollen ants then sick up the honeydew to feed the rest of the nest. Awful!

4 South American trapjaw ants have huge long jaws. (Well, they're huge by ant standards.) They catch little jumping insects called springtails in their jaws and then inject them with poison. But what's really awesome about these ants is that they also carry their eggs, or larvae, in those gruesome jaws as gently as any mother carries her baby – isn't that nice!

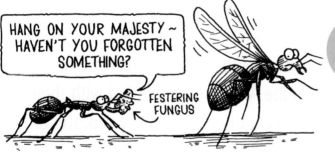

HANG ON YOUR MAJESTY ~ HAVEN'T YOU FORGOTTEN SOMETHING?

FESTERING FUNGUS

5 Leaf-cutter ants grow their own crops. The ants cut up the vegetation and mix it up with their droppings to make fertilizer. Then they grow fungus on it for food. They even weed unwanted kinds of fungus from their garden and put it on their compost heap. When a leaf-cutter queen leaves to start a new nest she always takes a bit of fungus with her to start a new garden.

6 And after the hard work of farming comes the harvest. Harvester ants live in the desert where they gather seed grains and make bread by chewing it all up and removing the husks. The ants store their bread until they get hungry.

LET'S STORE IT BEFORE IT TURNS TO TOAST!

7 The Australian bulldog ant has an awfully ugly bite. Not only is the bite painful, but this appalling ant then injects poison into the wound! Thirty stings can kill a human in 15 minutes. This is probably the most dangerous ant in the world...

8 Or is it? In the jungles of Africa and South America lurks something even more awesome. It's 100 metres long and 2 metres wide. It eats anything foolish enough to get in its way. It reduces lizards, snakes and even larger animals to skeletons. And even big strong humans run for their lives rather than face it. Nothing can fight against it and live. What is this terrifying creature? Is it an ant? Well yes, actually, it's a column of 20 million army ants. The ants have no settled home. They spend their time invading places and being awesomely awful to any creature that gets in their way. If you live in South America it could get rid of cockroaches in your home, but you'd have to get yourself out of the way first.

9 Red South American Amazon ants fight fierce battles against their deadly enemies – the black ants. Red ant foot patrols are sent out to find a way into the enemy nest. They leave a trail for the main army to follow. The main army attacks and the Amazon ants use their curved jaws to slice off the heads of the opposing black ants. Some of the Amazon ants spray gases to further confuse the black ants. Then the Amazon ants retreat with their prisoners – the black ant grubs. The grubs quickly pick up the smell of the Amazon ants and this fools them into thinking they're red ants too! But they aren't, and the poor befuddled black ants spend the rest of their lives as slaves to the awesome Amazon ants.

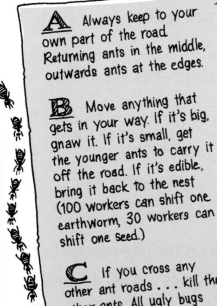

10 Marauder ants in Indonesia even build their own roads. These roads are often as long as 90 metres – and if you're ant-sized, that's awesome. Some of the roads even have soil roofs to protect them. And the ants have to follow a strict highway code:

Ant aromas

Scents are very important to ants. Scientists have discovered several ant scents each of which makes ants do different things. Imagine you were a scientist observing different kinds of ant behaviour. Could you match up the ant behaviour to the smell that causes it?

Here are some answers to get you started:
1 c) 2 g) 5 d).

See page 119 for the rest of the answers.

ALARM SMELL 1 — NEST SMELL 2 — TRAIL SMELL 3 — QUEEN BREEDING TIME SMELL 4 — BIG NASTY ENEMY SMELL 5 — DEAD ANT SMELL 6

a) THE ANTS TRY TO BURY YOU IN AN ANT CEMETERY

b) THE ANTS RUN AWAY FROM THEIR NEST

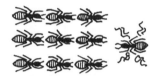

c) AN ANT ARMY IS SUMMONED

d) SOME ANTS TRY TO RUN AND OTHERS STAY TO FIGHT

e) ANTS FIGHT EACH OTHER

f) THE ANTS FIND THEIR WAY HOME

g) THE ANTS DON'T DO ANYTHING IF YOU HAVE THIS SMELL

h) MALE ANTS ARE ATTRACTED BY THIS SMELL

BET YOU NEVER KNEW!

There are 10,000 species of ant. But they do have some things in common.
- An ant nest is ruled by a queen who spends her life laying eggs.
- All the ordinary worker ants are female.
- Males only hatch out at mating time and they die once they have mated!

BARMY BEES

Ants and bees belong to the same gruesome group of ugly bugs. So it's no surprise to find some bee species live in nests ruled by queens. Humans tend to say that bees are "good" because they make honey – but bees can be bad in their own horrible way. You'll get a buzz (ha ha) out of teaching your teacher their ugly secrets.

Ugly bug fact file

NAME OF CREATURE: Bees and wasps

WHERE THEY LIVE: Worldwide. Most bees live on their own. Only a few species live in large nests.

HORRIBLE HABITS: They sting people.

ANY HELPFUL HABITS: Bees make honey and pollinate flowers.

DISTINGUISHING FEATURES: Thin waist between thorax and abdomen. Four transparent wings. Bees have long tongues and often carry yellow lumps of pollen on their hind legs.

WAIST

NASTY STINGY BIT

POLLEN

BEE

TONGUE

Inside the beehive

**Bees that live together in nests are called "social bees".
Well, you'd have to be social to live with this lot.**

QUARRELLING QUEENS Usually there's just one queen in a hive. She spends her time laying eggs. But sometimes more than one queen hatches out, and things can turn rather nasty. The first queen to appear kills off any rivals.

DROWSY DRONES It's a lovely life for a drone. Your worker sisters keep house for you. And they even feed you. You don't have a sting because you never need to fight anyone. There's just one problem. You've got to battle with hundreds of brothers for a chance to mate. If you mate with a queen you die.

WEARY WORKERS What do the workers do? Well (funnily enough) they work. And they work. And they work. In a few short weeks the worn-out workers work themselves to death!

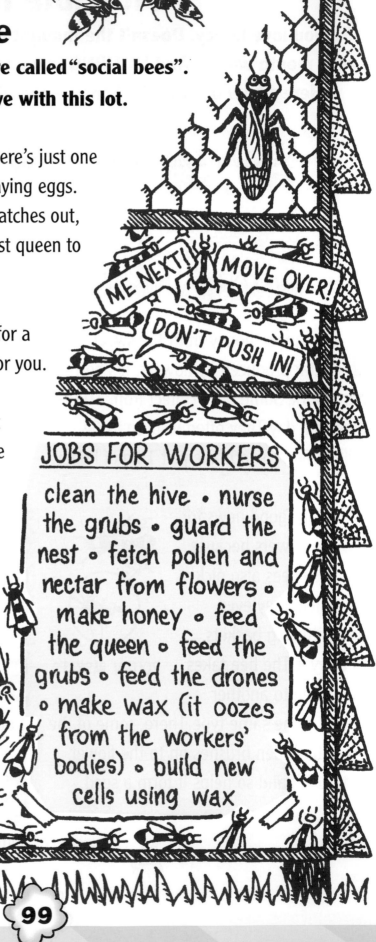

ME NEXT!

MOVE OVER!

DON'T PUSH IN!

JOBS FOR WORKERS

clean the hive • nurse the grubs • guard the nest • fetch pollen and nectar from flowers • make honey • feed the queen • feed the grubs • feed the drones • make wax (it oozes from the workers' bodies) • build new cells using wax

Horrible honey

So you love honey. Doesn't the thought of a lovely honey sandwich make your mouth water? And NOTHING is going to put you off it – right? RIGHT. Here's how bees make honey – complete with the horrible details.

1 Bees make honey from the sweet nectar produced by flowers. It's horribly hard work. Some bees collect from 10,000 flowers a day. They often visit up to 64 million flowers to make just 1 kg of honey.

2 That's good news for the flowers because the busy bees also pick up pollen. They even have little leg baskets to carry it. The bee takes the pollen to another flower of the same type. There, some of the precious pollen brushes on to the flower, fertilizes it and so helps it form a seed.

POLLEN BASKETS

3 Why do you think the flower goes to all the bother of making scents, bright colours and nectar. Is it all for us? No! It's to attract bees. Lots of bees means lots of flowers. See?

4 A bee uses her long tongue and a pump in her head to suck up nectar. She stores the nectar in a special stomach.

LONG SLIMY TONGUE

5 Nectar is mostly water. To get rid of the water, bees sick up the nectar and dry it out on their tongues – ugh.

6 Then they store the honey in honeycomb cells until they need it. That's unless humans steal it for their sandwiches!

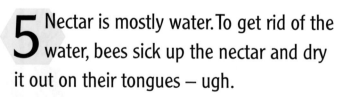

1 Put out a vase of flowers. Watch the bees find the flowers and go off to tell their friends.

"BUZZ

BUZZ

2 Meanwhile you hide the flowers.

3 Back come some more bees. They are humming with happiness at the thought of all that lovely nectar and pollen.

HAPPY BUZZ

4 But there are no flowers. Result: Bewildered bees.

???

BEEWILDER SOME BEES
It's best done on a summer's day in a garden or park where there are lots of bees.

BEES BEE-WARE
Bees have lots of horrible enemies. To stop them, every hive has its guards. The guards don't receive training but if they did it might look like this...

Honey-bee As long as they've got some food you let them in. If not, chase them away! Bee careful. Bees from other hives sometimes steal our honey!

Death's-head hawk moth This nastily-named night raider flies into our hive. It licks our lovely honey with its terribly long tongue. Bee on your guard after dark!

African honey-badger This hairy horror breaks open our honeycomb with its long claws. It makes shocking stinks to drive away our guards. STING ON SIGHT!

Blister-beetle grub Bee careful when you visit flowers. This greedy grub will ambush you! It hitches a free ride to our hive. Then it hides in our cells and guzzles our grubs.

Mouse Another horrible honey hunter. STING TO DEATH! Getting rid of the mouse's body is a bit of a bother. It's too big to move. Cover the body with gooey gum from trees. The gum will mummify the mouse and stop it stinking!

Humans They only want our honey and our bees' wax for polish and candles. Sting them if they get too close. You can't pull your sting from their skin. If you try it'll drag your insides out. Never mind - You'll die a heroine!

Cuckoo bee Don't be a cuckoo and let them in. It's easy to think they're one of us. But once inside they'll lay their ugly eggs.

The ugly inside story

We cut this cute little bee in half to find out how its body ticks.

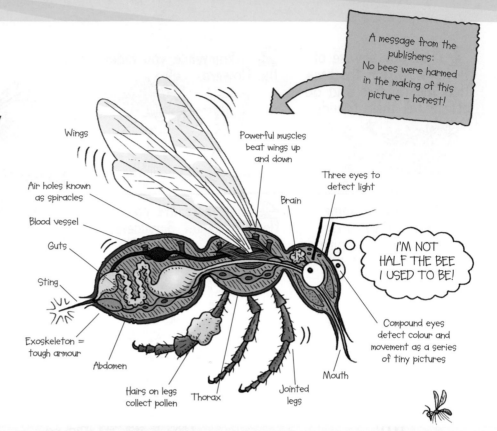

A message from the publishers: No bees were harmed in the making of this picture – honest!

Wings

Powerful muscles beat wings up and down

Three eyes to detect light

Brain

Air holes known as spiracles

Blood vessel

Guts

Sting

Exoskeleton = tough armour

Abdomen

Hairs on legs collect pollen

Thorax

Jointed legs

Mouth

Compound eyes detect colour and movement as a series of tiny pictures

I'M NOT HALF THE BEE I USED TO BE!

DARE YOU DISCOVER... Why bees store their honey in six-sided cells

WHAT YOU NEED:
- 3 A4 sheets of card ● 3 A4 sheets of squared paper ● Pencil
- Sticky tape and scissors

WHAT YOU DO:
1. Fold the first sheet of card in three and then fold it half. This will give you six equal sections. Fold the second sheet three times and fold the third sheet in half and then in half again.
2. Stick the ends of the first sheet together and shape it into a six-sided shape (hexagon) as shown. In the same way, make the second sheet into a triangle and the third sheet into a square.
3. Place each shape on a sheet of squared paper and draw around it.
4. Count the squares inside the shapes.

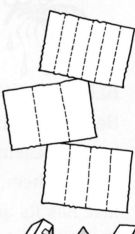

HMMM!

YOU SHOULD FIND:
There are more squares inside the hexagon. Bees make the cells they use to store honey and larvae using wax from their bodies. They don't want to waste wax so they use a shape that gives them the most storage space. Can you bee-lieve it?

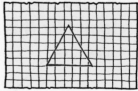

WICKED WORDSEARCH

Can you find all 15 horrible words in the gruesome grid below?
They might read up, down, forwards, backwards or diagonal.

a	t	e	n	r	o	h	e	l	s	y	f	w	g	c
i	m	q	u	y	m	p	t	b	g	s	i	a	e	k
d	h	b	e	e	t	w	v	r	a	w	l	n	s	o
e	k	u	b	h	s	y	m	c	p	o	o	q	u	y
c	a	t	e	r	p	i	l	l	a	r	c	s	n	a
q	l	t	n	y	c	a	j	y	d	k	a	m	l	o
w	u	e	i	h	l	u	f	a	i	e	n	n	a	d
p	h	r	a	t	c	e	n	a	o	r	l	h	r	o
e	o	f	r	w	r	i	r	d	s	a	h	i	v	e
r	i	l	r	f	n	d	t	p	h	e	g	h	a	u
n	e	y	l	v	s	e	i	o	s	o	m	e	e	g
k	r	t	n	e	u	f	h	m	r	a	i	e	p	z
f	n	v	g	a	n	l	d	j	b	s	w	b	l	z
b	j	r	z	c	r	y	e	n	o	h	n	x	h	u
q	u	e	e	n	o	s	i	h	p	v	j	t	d	b

bee

butterfly

buzz

caterpillar

drone

fly

hive

honey

hornet

larvae

nectar

pollen

queen

wasp

worker

See page 120 for the answers.

105

SINISTER SPIDERS

If ugly bugs look set to take over your home – don't despair.
Help is at hand! There are more than 36,000 spider species.
This one's the most common in homes. You might find it swimming
in your soup or scaring your sister in the bath.

INSTANT EXPERT: THE HOUSE SPIDER

CLOSE-UP OF HEAD

Spinnerets produce silk for web

Abdomen – you'll find spider guts in here

Little tube where spiders hide

Head

Jaw structure

Poison fangs

Cephalothorax (cef–fal–lo–thor–ax). Imagine that your head was part of your chest and you'll get the idea

FANCY BEING POISONED AND HAVING YOUR GUTS SUCKED OUT?

Sensory palps

NO FANGS!

Mouldy dead fly with its insides sucked out

HORRIBLE HEALTH WARNING!

It's common in Europe and North America. If you live in parts of Australia you might share your home with a black spider. Bites from this spider can cause swelling and vomiting. So don't make friends with it!

Every horrible scientist knows that flies get stuck to spider webs. And then the spider grabs the fly and injects poison through its fearsome fangs. The victim can't move. The sinister spider vomits digestive juices over its living victim and slurps the soupy goo. But what about spider family life? Surely they have a caring side? Read on and find out!

House spider webs are horribly untidy

House spider family life - A report by PC Beetle

I called at the house spider residence after complaints that the Spiders were a 'problem family.' In response to my questions Mrs Spider admitted that she hadn't seen her husband since last autumn. 'He stayed for a bite,' she admitted. 'I might have eaten him by mistake.' According to Mrs Spider her husband died of natural causes. I am not so sure...

Mrs Spider told me that her babies were living with her. 'They don't get on too well – in fact they keep eating each other. I'm glad they're moving to their own webs', she said. She then asked me to stick around for supper. At this point I tried to leave but I couldn't...

BET YOU NEVER KNEW!

This is happy families by Australian social spider standards. The spider mum lets her babies suck her blood. When she's too weak to move, they sick up digestive juices and turn her into mush and slurp up the revolting remains. I bet the babies say 'our mum makes a lovely tea!'

TEACHER'S TEA-BREAK TEASER

Bang on the staffroom door. When it opens, show your teacher your pet spider and ask...

WHY DOESN'T BERTIE STICK TO HIS WEB?

YARRRGH!

STAFFR

Answer on page 121

SAVAGE SPIDERS

The horrible thing about spiders is that you can't get away from them.
You can see their webs on plants and washing lines and in garden sheds.
And when you come home you'll probably find spiders hiding there too.
Spiders aren't insects but that doesn't make them any less horrible.
Maybe it's because spiders have some seriously savage habits.

Ugly bug fact file

NAME OF CREATURE: Spider

WHERE THEY LIVE: Worldwide. On land and in fresh water.

HORRIBLE HABITS: Paralyses prey with poison fangs and sucks out the juices.

ANY HELPFUL HABITS: Keeps down the numbers of insects.

DISTINGUISIHING FEATURES: Head and thorax joined. Separate abdomen. Four pairs of jointed legs. Eight eyes. Produces silk. Inside is a breathing organ called a book lung.

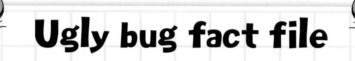

SEPARATE ABDOMEN

EIGHT HORRIBLE HAIRY LEGS

EYES

HEAD AND CHEST JOINED

Savage Spider File

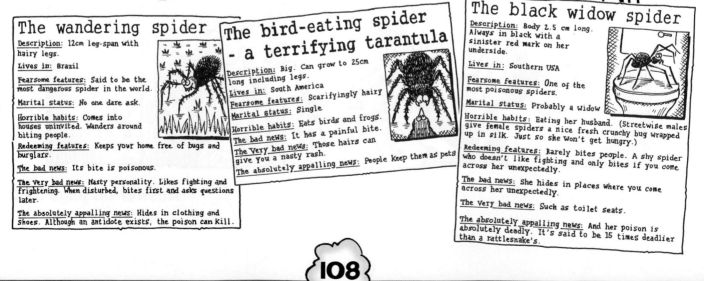

The wandering spider

Description: 12cm leg-span with hairy legs.

Lives in: Brazil

Fearsome features: Said to be the most dangerous spider in the world.

Marital status: No one dare ask.

Horrible habits: Comes into houses uninvited. Wanders around biting people.

Redeeming features: Keeps your home free of bugs and burglars.

The bad news: Its bite is poisonous.

The very bad news: Nasty personality. Likes fighting and frightening. When disturbed, bites first and asks questions later.

The absolutely appalling news: Hides in clothing and shoes. Although an antidote exists, the poison can kill.

The bird-eating spider - a terrifying tarantula

Description: Big. Can grow to 25cm long including legs.

Lives in: South America

Fearsome features: Scarifyingly hairy

Marital status: Single

Horrible habits: Eats birds and frogs.

The bad news: It has a painful bite.

The very bad news: Those hairs can give you a nasty rash.

The absolutely appalling news: People keep them as pets

The black widow spider

Description: Body 2.5 cm long. Always in black with a sinister red mark on her underside.

Lives in: Southern USA

Fearsome features: One of the most poisonous spiders.

Marital status: Probably a widow

Horrible habits: Eating her husband. (Streetwise males who doesn't like fighting give female spiders a nice fresh crunchy bug wrapped up in silk. Just so she won't get hungry.)

Redeeming features: Rarely bites people. A shy spider who doesn't like fighting and only bites if you come across her unexpectedly.

The bad news: She hides in places where you come across her unexpectedly.

The very bad news: Such as toilet seats.

The absolutely appalling news: And her poison is absolutely deadly. It's said to be 15 times deadlier than a rattlesnake's.

Quick Quiz

1 **How do spiders avoid getting caught in their own webs?**

a) Nifty footwork.

b) They have oily non-stick feet.

c) They slide down a line and pulley.

EIGHT WALKING STICKS - HE MUST BE OLD!

2 **How long can a spider live?**

a) Six months **b)** 25 years **c)** 75 years

3 **When a spider sheds its skin what parts does it get rid of?**

a) Its skin.

b) The front of its eyes

c) The lining of its guts and book lung (breathing organ).

4 **What does a spider do with its old web?**

a) Wear its. **b)** Throws it away. **c)** Eats it.

5 **How do small spiders fly through the air?**

a) They use electriciy in the atmosphere.

b) They inflate their bodies like tiny balloons.

c) They spin little silk parachutes.

6 **What does a spitting spider do?**

a) It spits a poison that kills its victims as they try to escape.

b) It lassoes its victims with a 10-cm squirt of silk that ties them to the ground.

c) Nothing. It sits around looking strangely sinister.

SPLOT

AARGHH

7 **What, according to legend, is the best way to cure the bite of a tarantula spider?**

a) A cup of tea.

b) A lively folk dance.

c) Suck out the venom.

8 **How many spiders are there in one square metre of grassland?**

a) 27 **b)** 500 **c)** 1,795

9 **How does a spider get into your bath?**

a) It crawls up the drainpipe but can't climb out of the bath.

b) It drops down from the ceiling but can't climb out of the bath.

c) It crawls out of the taps but can't climb out of the bath.

Answers on page 121

Weird webs

Spiders spin silk to produce their intricate webs. The webs they make catch flies and other unlucky creatures. But the more you find out about webs the weirder they seem.

1 To make one web, spiders need to spin different types of silk.

• Dry silk a thousandth of a millimetre thick for the spokes of a web.

• Stretchy silk covered in gluey droplets for the rest. The sticky bits take in moisture and stop the web drying out.

• Other kinds of silk for wrapping up eggs and dead insects.

SHUT THE DOOR, LOVE – THERE'S A TERRIBLE DRAUGHT COMING DOWN THE TUNNEL!

2 Webs come in many shapes and sizes. Have you ever seen any of these?

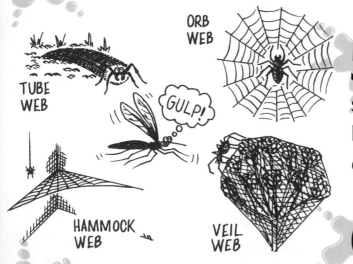

ORB WEB

TUBE WEB

GULP!

HAMMOCK WEB

VEIL WEB

3 The house spider makes a hammock-shaped web. The spider spits out bits of insect and leaves them lying around for someone else to tidy up – a horrible habit!

4 The trap-door spider digs a tunnel with a trap door at one end. The spider waits within. It grabs a passing insect and pulls it down. The door closes and the innocent victim is never seen again.

5 The purse-web spider makes a purse-shaped web. This savage spider then stabs its victims through the web with its long poison fangs. Then before settling down to dinner it carefully repairs the tear.

6 Sinister nephila (nef-illa) spiders spin giant webs up to 2 metres across to catch insects and sometimes even birds. And even fish aren't safe – in the early part of this century people in New Guinea used the silk to make fishing nets!

7 The web-throwing spider chucks its web over insects as they work under its hiding place. Then the spider drops in for tea.

8 When an insect gets caught in a spider's web, it struggles and the vibrations alert the spider. But the devious ero spider manages to sneak on to its enemy's web and bite the spider before it even realizes its got a visitor. Evil ero then sucks its victim dry and scurries away, leaving an empty spider husk sitting in its web!

9 In some places in California, spiders' webs fall like snow. The flakes are made up of mixed-up spiders' webs blown together by the wind.

And now you know all about these hairy horrors...

DARE YOU make friends with ... a spider?

To save spinning your own silk, try asking a spider to make some for you.

WHAT YOU NEED:
- A plastic bottle ● Soil and twigs ● Pencil
- Sticky tape and scissors

WHAT YOU DO:
Cut a plastic lemonade bottle in half. (Get an adult to help you.)

Add soil and twigs to the bottom half.

Now find your spider. Sheds and out-houses are good places to look. If you find a web the spider is normally hiding nearby. One spider is enough. Add two and one will eat the other! Be gentle, though – spiders are easily hurt!

Tape up the two halves of the bottle.

Feed your new friend with a small fly through the top of the bottle.

YOU SHOULD FIND:
Check to see if she's spun any silk or made a web. If she has, go ahead and try knitting yourself a nice pair of spider silk gloves.

UGLY BUGS VS HORRIBLE HUMANS

Since the day that a caveman or cavewoman first squashed a cockroach there has been a non-stop war between ugly bugs and humans. It's the biggest war the world has ever known.

You might think that humans have an advantage over insects. A human is far bigger than the biggest insect. So humans can easily squash them. Humans are more intelligent than insects. (Well, most humans are!) But if you look at what humans and insects can do for their size the picture is very different.

Ugly Bug Olympics

RUNNING

Winner: One species of cockroach can run 50 times its body length in one second.

Loser: The fastest human to run 50 times his own body length (about 80 metres) was about nine times slower.

THE HIGH JUMP

Winner: Fleas can jump 30 cm – that's 130 times their own height.

Loser: To match that a human would have to jump 250 metres into the air!

THE LONG JUMP

HUMAN — FEEBLE HOP!

INSECT

Winner: Jumping spiders can leap 40 times their body length.

Runner-up: Grasshoppers can leap 20 times their own body length.

Loser: To match that a human would have to leap the length of nine London buses in a single jump!

WEIGHT-LIFTING

GET THEM OFF ME!

HUMAN

INSECT

Winner: Scarab beetles can lift weights 850 times heavier than their own bodies.

Loser: To equal that a human would have to lift eight London buses at the same time!

WALKING ON THE CEILING

AAHHHH

HUMAN

SO THAT'S FIVE GOLD MEDALS FOR THE BEAUTIFUL BUGS

INSECT

Winner: Flies.

Loser: Humans can't do this at all.

HO RIBLE HUMANS HIT BACK

Day after day humans wage war against insects with every weapon at their disposal. But they've also discovered some surprisingly horrible uses for insects and other ugly bugs.

REVOLTING RECIPES

If you can't dispose of ugly bugs you could always eat them. That's what millions of apparently sane people do throughout the world. Would you want to try any of these dishes?

Sweets

Mexican honeypot ants
A sweet sticky treat.

Baked bee and wasp grubs
An old recipe from Somerset in England. Juicy grubs baked in hot sticky honeycomb.

After your meal
Try one of our tarantula-fang toothpicks as used by the Piaroa people of Venezuela.

Starters

Fried and salted termites
An African treat. Tastes like fried pork rind, peanuts and potato chips all mixed up!

L'escargots
Oui, mes amis! The traditional French delicacy. (Snails to you.) Fed on lettuce. Boiled and cooked with garlic, butter, shallots, salt, pepper and lemon juice. Served with parsley. Bon appetit!

Fried witchetty grub
A native Australian delicacy – these are giant wood-moth grubs. They look a bit like fusilli pasta and swell up when fried. Delicious!

Main courses

Stir-fried silkworm pupae
This tasty traditional Chinese dish is prepared with garlic, ginger, pepper and soy sauce. Wonderful warm nutty custard flavour. You spit out the shells. Very good for high blood pressure.

Roast longhorn timber beetle
Deliciously crunchy balsawood flavour. As cooked by the native people of South America.

Fried Moroccan grasshopper
Boiled bug bodies prepared with pepper, salt and chopped parsley then fried in batter with a little vinegar. You can also eat them raw.

Blue-legged tarantula
A popular spider dish in Laos in South-east Asia. Freshly toasted and served with salt or chillies. Flavour similar to the marrow in chicken bones.

Ugly bugs vs horrible humans: the debate

For every argument there are two points of view. And this is certainly true for ugly bugs and humans. See for yourself. Who do you sympathize with most – ugly bugs or humans?

Human point of view	Ugly bug point of view
Ugly bugs sting and bite us.	Humans trap us, poison us and experiment on us.
Ugly bugs eat our crops.	Humans destroy our food plants and plant their crops too close together so we've got nothing else to eat.
Ugly bugs creep into our homes.	Humans destroy <u>our</u> homes.
Ugly bugs spread diseases.	Humans spread pollution and rubbish.
Ugly bugs destroy our furniture.	To us it's only wood.
Ugly bugs cost us money.	Who cares about money?
They destroy our property.	Who cares about property?

Ugly bugs just want the same things we want. Nice food and somewhere to live. The problem only comes when their idea of nice food is your nice food, and their idea of somewhere to live is your bedroom.

ANSWERS

p.9 Beastly basics quiz

1 Carnivores
2 The winged warrior defends its habitat by pooing on trespassers!
3 Dead animals
4 Crocodiles
5 They have no ears
6 The poor mites suffer from sunburn
7 Polar bears
8 The plant eaters would increase their numbers and guzzle all the plants until they ran out of food. Then they would die out.

p.10 Odd one out

D) is the odd one out

p.13 Weird wildlife quiz

1 Probably false, although some people swear they've seen it. Maybe it's a relative of the more famous Loch Ness Monster. The Swedish government has banned attempts to kill or capture the creature just in case it does exist.
2 True. The horn is 15 cm long. The bird itself lives in marshes in tropical South America. You can hear its scream 3 km (2 miles) away.
3 True.
4 False.
5 True. The golden tree snake can glide 46 metres. The snake launches itself from a high branch and draws its underside in and pushes its body forward as it zooms through the air.

6 True. It uses its fins to grab branches. Once in the trees it allows ants to crawl over its body. Then it leaps back in the river. The ants fall off the fish and float around in the water – to be gobbled at leisure!
7 False.
8 True. It's the duck-billed platypus! This strange creature is actually an unusual species of mammal that looks like a mole pretending to be a duck. The puzzling platypus has also got detectors that sense electrical waves given off by small creatures at the bottom of muddy rivers. Classifying this freaky creature could drive a naturalist quackers.

p.25 Savage shark survival quiz

1 c) The lifeguard could help you. Anywhere with juicy dead fish or seals is going to be a magnet for great whites.
2 c) Experts call yellow "yum-yum yellow" because the colour seems to attract sharks. They could mistake the stripes for a stripy fish. The armour is a bad choice because it causes electrical currents that sharks sense. Oh yes – and you could sink to the bottom of the sea and drown. Mind you, shark scientists do wear a kind of armour called chain-mail to protect themselves against smaller sharks.
3 a) Shampoo contains sodium lauryl sulphate – a chemical that puts sharks off when you squirt it into their mouths. I expect

116

they "hair off" in the opposite direction. The bomb could injure a shark and make it more dangerous. In the 1950s US scientists tried to train Simo the dolphin to fight sharks, but scared Simo scarpered from larger sharks. Sounds like a sensible Simo to me.

4 c) The surfboard is seal-shaped when seen from underneath so it might draw sharks. Experiments by US scientist A. Peter Klimley show that sharks hate sheep so they won't eat it. It was a woolly-minded idea anyway…

5 b) If a shark grabs you, fighting back is your only chance.

WHAT YOUR SCORE MEANS

5 Shark survivor! You're clued up and know exactly what to do. There's NO WAY you'll end up as a shark snack!

3–4 Careful now! You made a few silly mistakes and you could be chancing your arm … or possibly your leg!

1–2 Accident waiting to happen. You've got it coming!

0 YOU'RE A DEAD LOSS! Well, dead actually.

p.29 Spot the difference

1 The crocodile has a more pointed snout.
2 You can see a lower tooth on each side of the croc's jaw.
3 The croc buries her eggs in a nest of sand. The alligator makes her nest from rotting plants.

p.32 "Can you believe it?" quiz

1 TRUE You'll be pleased to hear that the horse survived its injury and is now in a stable condition – geddit?

2 TRUE The crafty croc had crawled into the man's sleeping bag but another camper frightened it away.

3 TRUE Mac Bosco Chawinga was grabbed by the croc but escaped after biting its snout – and that's snout too funny if you're a croc.

4 TRUE The children tied the alligator up with clothes but I bet their teachers were terrified.

5 FALSE Alligators don't live in sewers although they can be swept into them by heavy rains. If the teacher had been bitten he'd have nipped in the toilet, been nipped on the toilet and nipped out even faster!

6 FALSE No croc ever had wings. Oh don't tell me you fell for that!!!

p.45 Spot the difference

p.49 Bear true or false quiz

1 TRUE – polar bears probably shake hands with their left paws, but other bears can be left- or right-handed.

2 FALSE – pink polar bears, ha ha – as if! No, the polar bear was dyed purple by an antiseptic spray. Now isn't that a colour to "dye" for?

3 TRUE – the blood vessel that goes to the brain is designed to lose heat to cooler veins heading in the opposite direction. Hot-headed bears also lose heat through their noses.

4 TRUE – bears don't poo or pee for six months when they're hibernating (sleeping through the winter). So how long can your teacher last? Hmm – on second thoughts, don't ask!

5 TRUE – pandas pee on trees to mark their territory. Standing on its front paws helps the panda pee higher and so fool other pandas that it's bigger. Don't try handstands in the toilet – they can result in unfortunate accidents!

6 FALSE – they have a kind of soggy doggy smell.

7 TRUE – but only if it's an adult bear. Their claws are the wrong shape for climbing.

p.55 Bears Beware! quiz
DO'S:

2 Bears can sniff out blood – and they think that an injured human might make an easy meal.

3 Feel free – the bears know where you are anyway and the sound might frighten them away. But if you manage to spot one before it sees you, you might want to stay quiet for fear of annoying it.

6 Slowly does it!

8 Grizzly bears lose interest but you might have to put up with one of them munching your leg if it's hungry. Try not to wriggle too much if that happens. Black bears might eat the rest of you so only pretend to be dead if you can't get away.

9 This is good advice when dealing with grizzlies, but black bears climb and if one rips your trousers off you could have a bear behind.

DON'TS

1 This is berry bad advice – the bears normally eat berries so they'll be hungry and more likely to attack.

4 Bears love chocolate and can sniff it out from a distance. Although the bear will happily accept your chocolate it might absent-mindedly walk off with your arm too.

5 The smell is bound to attract bears. If you've already eaten the hamburgers, they can smell the food on your clothes and breath.

7 In bear language this is like saying: "OI, CUP-CAKE, YOU LOOK LIKE MY TEDDY!"

10 This is when the females are most vicious.

p.64–65 Lion hunting tips

1 b)

2 a) Lions show a lot of teamwork when hunting. Some scientists believe that this is an illusion and all the lions are doing their own thing.

3 c)

4 b) Males are bigger and stronger than the females. If there's not enough food for everyone the lionesses and cubs starve.

5 c) Nasty but true. The male wants the lioness to look after his youngsters once they are born. The lioness wants the male to protect her from other males.

6 b) A starving lion will eat anything so be careful if you're in the area.

p.76 Incredible bug discoveries quiz

The made up places are...

c) There are no active volcanoes in Switzerland.

e) The heat of the light would kill any bugs or microbes.

The others are true...

a) Scientists have found strange new types of microbes living in the ice just above the lake and nicknamed them "Mickey Mouse" and "Klingon". The scientists believe that the water may be home to microbes that have been lost to the world for 25 million years.

b) The symbion (sim-be-on), first spotted in 1995, is just 1 mm (0.04 inches) long. In fact, people who eat lobsters have been scoffing the bugs for years without noticing!

d) The xeno (ze-no) is a tiny insect with 100 eyes. Despite all the studies of wasps over the years, no one noticed the xeno until 1995, but I guess the xeno's had its eyes on us.

Ugly bugs true and false quiz

1 TRUE. The course is just 30 cm (one foot) long.

2 FALSE

3 TRUE. They're particularly good at tasting sugar and in fact the fly's feet are many times better at tasting than your tongue.

4 TRUE. The female fly can sense grubs cowering beneath the bark. It drills its egg-laying tube through the wood and spears the grubs before laying its eggs inside their living bodies. The eggs hatch into ichneumon grubs and eat their hosts alive!

5 FALSE. The mysterious chocolate disappearances in your house may have something to do with your mum.

6 TRUE. The mouse-eating spider of South America rubs its legs hard to make a cloud of tiny hairs that stick in the flesh and cause a burning pain.

7 TRUE. The attacker eats the guts and the sea cucumber escapes to grow more guts. Yes – this fact is really hard to stomach!

8 TRUE. Believe it or not, she taught her spiders to spell the word "HI" in their webs and she has also taught a swarm of bees to land on top of her head in the shape of a hat. Maybe she's just got a bee in her bonnet...

p.97 Ant aromas

to get you started...

1 c) 2 g) 5 d)

missing answers...

3 f) 4 h) 6 a)

p.103 Wicked wordsearch

p.104-105 Scary Skies

p.107 Teacher's Tea Break Teaser

Scientists have been arguing about this for years. Even if your teacher knows the answer, it will take her ages to explain. Basically, not all web strands are sticky and the sensible spiders walk on the non-sticky threads. If they do tread on a blob of glue they free themselves with their claws.

p.109 Quick Quiz –

Savage Spiders

1 b)

2 b) Tarantulas can live this long.

3 All of these!

4 c)

5 c) Sometimes it's a length of silk and sometimes it's a silken loop that acts just like a parachute.

6 b)

7 b) A spider's bite is supposed to make you dance madly – that's called tarantism. The tarantella folk dance is supposed to cure the bite.

8 b) Scientists reckon there are two billion spiders in England and Wales!

9 b) The spider drops in for a drink of water. But the sides of the bath are too slippery for the spider to climb out again.

INDEX

alligators 29, 31, 32, 60, 117

amphibia 8

animals, sea 7, 8, 12, 20–27, 29, 40, 42, 77, 81, 89, 91, 119

animals, largest 12, 89, 91

animals, smallest 12

antelopes 64, 65, 71

ants 77, 79, 92, 94–97, 114, 116

aphids 95

arachnids (*see spiders*)

babies 17, 19, 48, 70–71

bacteria 18, 87

bats 38, 68, 74, 80, 93

bears 48–55, 63, 71, 116, 118

bees 79, 86, 98–105, 114

beetles 79, 86, 101, 113, 114

birds 8, 16, 17, 18, 28, 47, 62, 67, 68, 71, 72–73, 74, 89, 90, 108, 110, 116

bloodsuckers 16, 47, 82, 107

boa constrictors 38

butterflies 81, 87

camouflage 21, 56

carnivores (meat-eaters)

2–27, 28–33, 38–45, 49, 56–67, 89, 116

caterpillars 81, 87, 94

cats 14, 56–67, 69

centipedes 82, 86, 90

chameleons 8

classes of animals 6–8

claws 48, 56, 118, 121

cnidaria 7

cobras 39, 41

cockroaches 80, 112

crabs 7, 47, 82

crepuscular creatures 48–55

crickets 79, 93

crocodiles 28–33, 36, 46, 70, 116, 117

crustacea 7

deer 56

direction-finding 72, 73

dogs 8, 19, 68

dolphins 25, 27, 117

dragonflies 81

drawing horrible animals 34–37, 74–75, 86–87

ducks 8, 74

eagles 17, 68, 74

earthquakes 69

earwigs 78

echidnas 18

echinoderms 7

eggs 8, 17, 21, 28, 39, 70, 73, 89, 95, 97, 99, 101, 110, 119

electricity 18, 69, 109, 116

elephants 37, 60

farting 20

fish 7, 12, 19, 20–27, 28, 42, 65, 68, 69, 70, 73, 93, 110, 116

fleas 16, 87, 112

flies 75, 77, 80, 81, 106, 110, 113, 119

flying 71, 72, 79, 80

food webs 17

foxes 16, 17

frogs 8, 17, 19, 63, 70, 108

gills 7, 20

giraffes 37

gorillas 14–15

grasshoppers 17, 79, 113, 114

habitats 17

hedgehogs 90

herbivores (plant-eaters) 9, 116

hibernation 51

honey 98–101, 114

honey-badgers 101

horses 32, 117
humans 8, 19, 32, 101
hummingbirds 12, 75
hyenas 17, 59, 62

insects 63, 65, 66, 70, 73,
    76–81, 83, 86,
    94–105, 108, 110,
    111, 112–113
invertebrates 9

jaguars 57
jellyfish 7, 27, 46

kittens 14, 60, 67

leaf insects 79
leeches 82, 86
legs 7, 30, 48, 52, 66, 74,
    75, 78, 81, 82, 83, 87,
    98, 100, 102, 108, 119
leopards 57, 59
lice 80, 87
Linnaeus, Carl (Swedish
    scientist) 6
lions 36, 56, 58, 59, 60,
    62, 64, 118–119
lobsters 7, 82, 119

maggots 76, 87
mammals 8, 12, 28, 48–55,
    56–67, 116
mice 65, 67, 69, 101, 119
millipedes 82, 83
mites 82, 84–85, 87
molluscs 81
mongooses 63
monkeys 36, 38, 57

moths 81, 101, 114

omnivores (eat anything)
    48–55

parrots 74, 84
pee 46, 49, 58, 118
penguins 70, 74
pigeons 72–73
plants 17, 18
platypuses, duck-billed 116
poison 7, 39–40, 42,
    43–44, 46, 95, 106,
    108, 109, 110, 115
pollen 98, 100, 103
poo 19, 49, 50, 85, 93,
    116, 118
praying mantises 80
pythons 38

rabbits 16, 17, 18, 67, 68
rats 19, 47, 67
rattlesnakes 39, 40, 63, 108
reptiles 8, 28–33, 38–45

scorpions 7
sea cucumbers 77, 119
seals 20, 25, 27, 63, 69
senses
    hearing 68, 72, 116
    sight 68, 69, 72, 102, 116
    smell 48, 64, 68, 77,
        97, 118, 119
    taste 68, 77, 119
    touch 69
sharks 20–27, 116
sheep 25, 177
siphonophores 27

skeletons 7, 20
skin 7, 8, 28, 37, 42, 70,
    84, 109
slugs 77, 81, 83, 86, 88,
    90–91, 92, 93
snails 81, 83, 86, 88–89,
    114
snakes 8, 16, 17, 19, 37,
    38–45, 62, 116
spiders 7, 77, 82, 83, 86,
    106–111, 113, 119,
    121
starvation 47, 119
stings 7, 98, 99, 101,
    102, 115

tarantulas 108, 109, 114,
    121
teeth 28, 48, 56, 67, 89
termites 79, 93, 114
tigers 56, 58, 60, 62
toads 8, 70
tortoises 8, 65
tree-climbing 12, 47, 49,
    59, 71, 116, 118

vipers 39, 46

wasps 76, 79, 98, 114, 119
webs 106, 108, 109, 110–
    111, 121
whales 12
wings 47, 74, 79, 80, 81,
    83, 98, 102
woodlice 82, 83, 93
worms 82, 83, 86, 89, 90,
    93

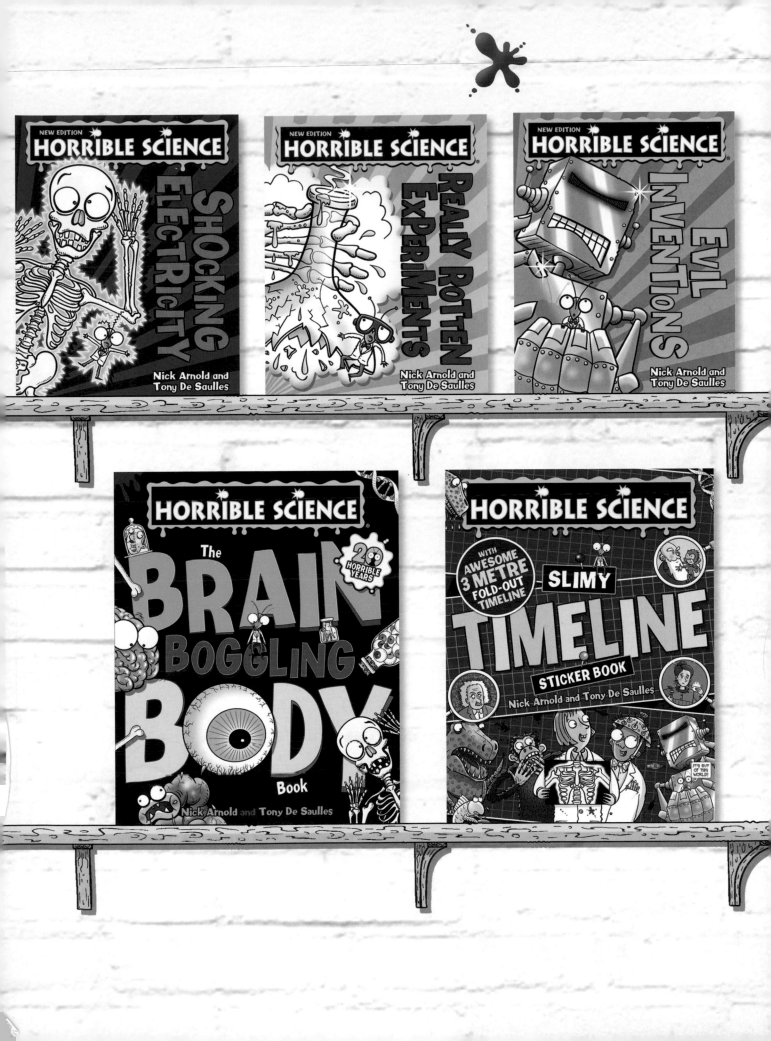